I0397207

DON'T LET THE HURT...
...MAKE YOU BITTER,
BE A REFLECTION OF THE "SON'.

DON'T LET THE HURT...
...MAKE YOU BITTER,
BE A REFLECTION OF THE "SON'.

VOLUME ONE
(INSPIRATIONAL/ANTHOLOGY)

REVISED EDITION

Written and Illustrated by:

Nevaeh J. M. Sapphire

COPYRIGHT

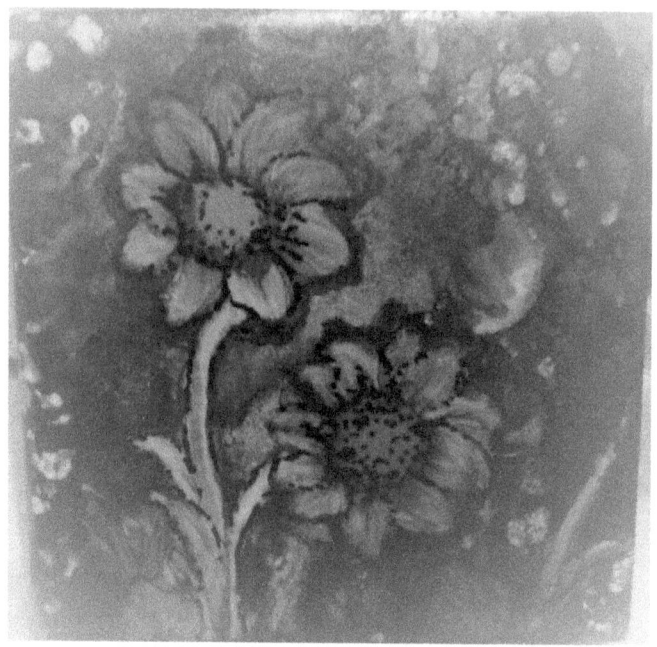

"Plant Seeds of Love Along Your Path"
-alcohol ink

Disclaimer: This revised edition has not been professionally edited.
*Copying any part of this book, by any form is prohibited unless written permission is given by the author.
Copyright 2019
ISBN: 9781092298230

DEDICATION

*To my Precious Children, (Josh, Olivia and Curt)

The love Jesus and I have for you is unconditional, never forget that! There are NO favorites between the three of you! From my childhood to my adulthood my parents shared stories of their childhood which impacted my life in so many ways. Some mothers have said, they wrote letters to their children, these books are my letters to the three of you. May these writings impact your lives in more ways than one!!! My advice to you is to seek God, keep Him first, recognize and KNOW His voice! I have often said mothering is the hardest job in the world yet the most rewarding! I pray for you all daily, believing one day we will be together forever.

1 Corinthians 2:5 "That your faith should not stand in the wisdom of men, but in the power of God." This is a very powerful scripture I have had to recall so many times. Mankind will let us down, but God will not!!! Therefore, we need to look at our brethren as brethren not placing any of them on a pedestal for, they too are human

and will fail. Forgive them and love all mankind! We need to seek God for our answers. He will not misdirect us if we fully trust Him and patiently wait for His guidance. If I get there before you do, I will be waiting...
I LOVE YOU!
Mom

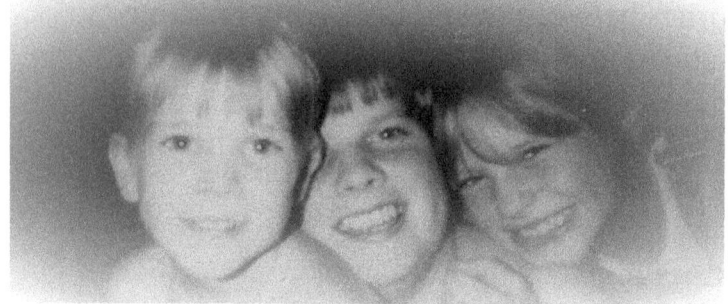

John 16:21 "A woman when she is in travail hath sorrow, because her hour is come: but as soon as she is delivered of the child, she remembereth no more the anguish, for joy that a man is born into the world."

*To my parents, who I love so dear and cannot thank enough for all the support over the years. After becoming a parent, myself, I realized how much effort went into your parenting and the many sacrifices you both made for us. Thank you for teaching me the importance of prayer!

*To my siblings, I may have been the baby of the family however your experiences have taught me many lessons about life!

*To all my lifetime friends who have been like siblings to me. You are the kind of friends that we can pick up where we left off, no matter the time or distance. Oh, the laughs… the memories…

~~~

Acknowledgement

Thank you to those who proofread and gave me feedback! Your input has made these books complete. One reader replied, "Needs a little more seasoning, a little more personal stories" thus you will find seasoning sprinkled within, in the form of humor along with personal stories. Another reader stated, "There's a lot of preaching in this book."

A special Thanks to a lady who has exemplified what "a true friend" means. I think of all the times she has come to my rescue and this time was no different! She is like a sister from another mother. She took the time to critique my manuscripts, corrected the punctuation and grammar mistakes. Also made suggestions in the areas that needed improvement. When I heard her say, "This is book worthy." WOW, how I was finally able to exhale an eager pocket of air!!!

Hats off to another dear friend, who proofread, edited and left sticky notes throughout the book. She kindly identified my lack of grammar skills and the love I have for run on sentences. Among her notes was a letter I cherish. Some quotes from her letter were: "Through your book, God spoke to my spirit." "You could not have written a better title." (The title was given by the Holy Spirit.)

When a writer decides to publish his or her work, allowing the door to be opened for the world to walk inside one's inner being, it is like a gamble. The writer may be a novice, such as myself. Therefore, one must be ready for critics or scoffers to pick apart her form of expressing herself. One must be ready to handle opinions as well as positive feedback not becoming prideful or arrogant. Although the goal is not only to tell my story but to open a door of opportunity, a challenge, per se for one to become a different person, closer to God.

As I was proofreading, I felt the Holy Spirit reminding me of the times I have heard preachers or evangelists say, "This sermon isn't just for you but for me as well!" So, as you read each topic remember they were also sent for me. It is not my intent to paint a façade, I have failed many times and still fail. Honestly, I am guilty of being rebellious for example not studying and reading like I should. I am not the person I used to be nor am I the person I want to be, however I am determined to become her!

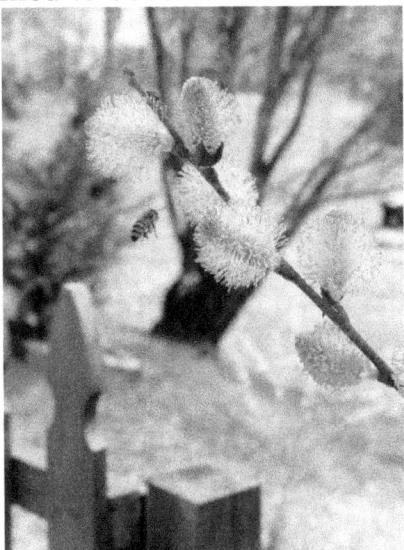

"Bee-Determined"
"Blessed are they which do hunger and thirst after righteousness: for they shall be filled."
Matthew 5.6

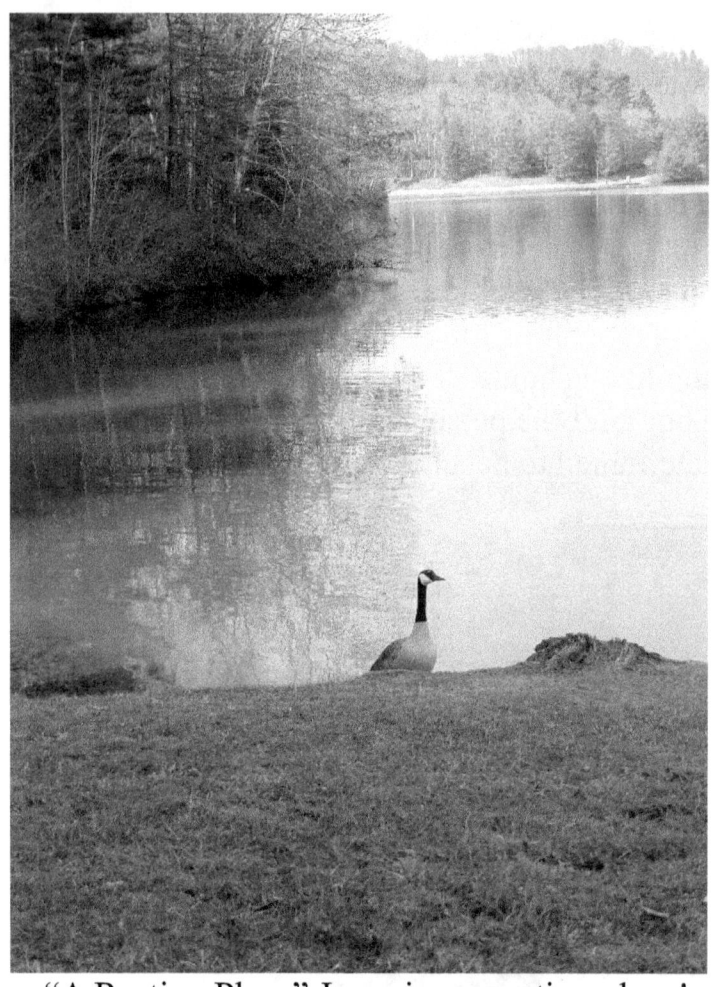

"A Resting Place" Jesus is my resting place!
"Those things, which ye have both learned, and
received, and heard, and seen in me, do: and the
God of peace shall be with you." Phillipians 4:9

Table of Content

Volume One: Overcoming Life's Challenges Through Christ

~Inspirational thoughts, valuable lessons learned ...and still learning

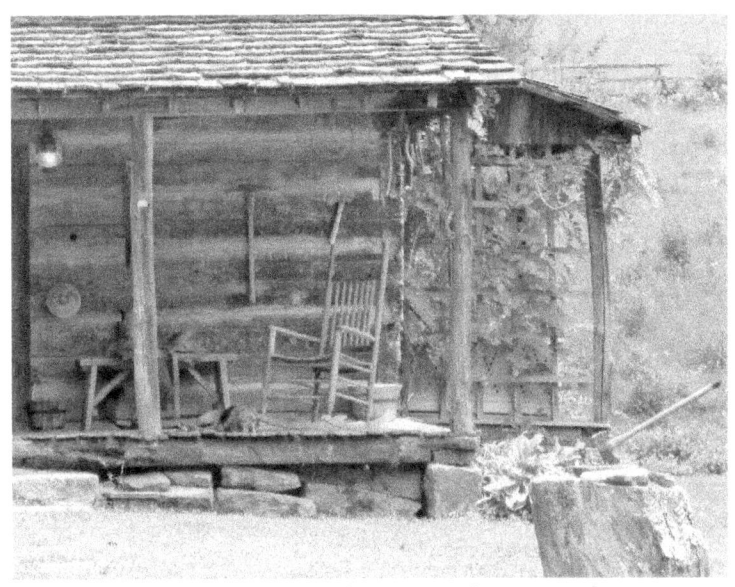

"Chores… Laughter… The Evening
Conversations…

FORWARD

Volume One begins a series of books, written by
an author who has learned to overcome life's
challenges through Christ. In this book, she
shares insights, humor, valuable lessons learned
and how to transform one's hurt/bitterness into
triumphs. After becoming a widow during her
midlife and after years of being a single mom
she found beauty among the ashes through
ministry and art. This is an inspirational
collection of heart felt narratives from
overcoming fears, learning self-control to the
battle of weight loss. This book contains poetry,
artwork, quilts, and photography which are all
God given talents that often helped with the
offset when there was more month than money.
Nevaeh, a mother of three, also a grandmother of
three shares many topics common to us all. She
suggests ways to improve relationships not only
between a male and female but one's relationship
with Christ. Inside this book, you will find a
narrative titled, "A Marriage License is Not an
Owner's Permit" hoping to improve and restore
marriages! Volume One is a prelude to Volume
Two and Three. Volume Two is a memoir she
has written from her wonderful memories of

motherhood to recalling her childhood as a coal miner's daughter; from dealing with drug addiction within her family to speaking up for those who can't through advocating for her son. Volume Three depicts a span of time between two sisters as cancer invades their timeline. Cancer is not just a word or illness...

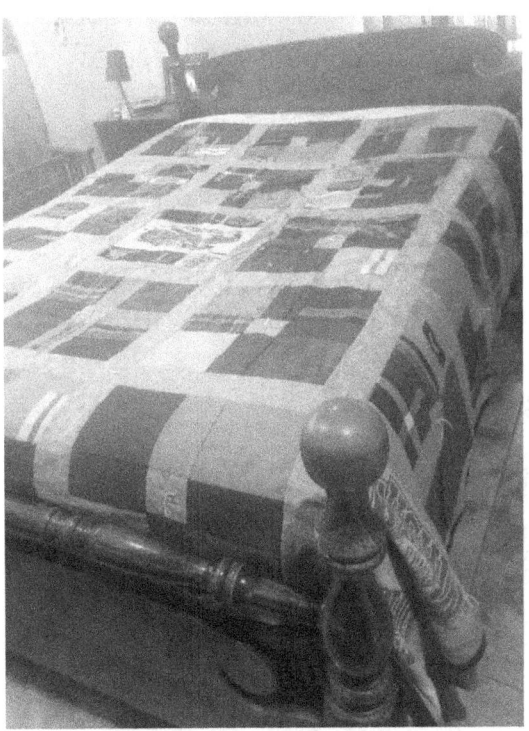

"In Memory of a Coal Miner"
The first memory quilt I made. Thanks, Kathy, for the photo.

Cover Page

The cover of this book was a photo I had taken, while at one of my favorite places to visit in West Virginia. A place where the fresh, seemingly undisturbed morning air and solitude were greatly appreciated! The view from the bottoms of the enormously tall hardwoods, some which were tagged; the unusual breed of flowers, unsure how many were on the endangered list; and the sights and sounds of animals made for a rejuvenating getaway. Among the many photos, I chose this photo because of the serenity there, a quiet place to meditate and be alone with God surrounded by His artwork/creations. This was a solemn place to recharge!

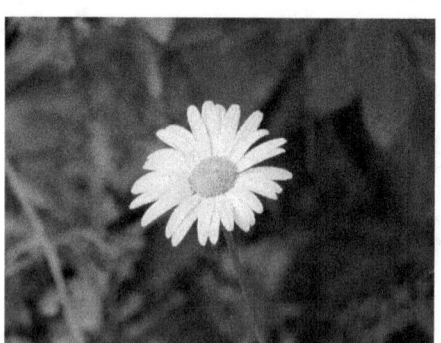

"He loves me, He loves me not?
...OH, HE DEFINITELY LOVES ME!

PREFACE

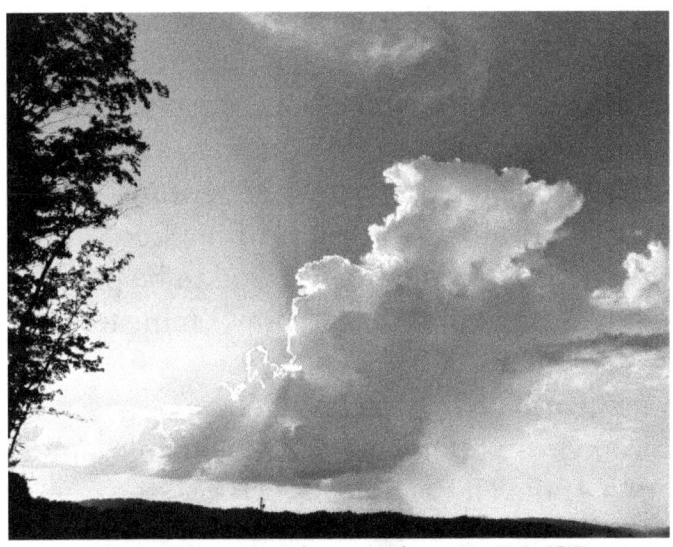

"Son-Rays" -Photo taken at BMSP

Father, You, know our insecurities, fears and hurt, may we see just a ray of Your "Son-light" to help us overcome? Lord, it is through Your Word we gain not only wisdom but strength and the ability to forgive! The scripture, John 3:17 tells us, Jesus did not come to condemn us but to save us.

As you read this book, may you let go of the hurt and/or guilt, forgive others as well as self! May you be inspired to find Jesus Christ amidst your hurt and allow His love to embrace, comfort, and redefine you! For we all have a past, and He is the only hope we have. Not only in this present day, but our only hope for an eternal home. 1 Cor. 1:9 "GOD is faithful..."

May you allow these books, especially Volume One to minister to you, I am still in awe how God ministered to me while writing. As Christians we all are ministers of the Lord in some form or fashion. I want God to be pleased with how I lived my life and how I ministered, don't you?

*Some names have been changed.
*Scriptures are referenced from the King James Version of the <u>Holy Bible.</u>

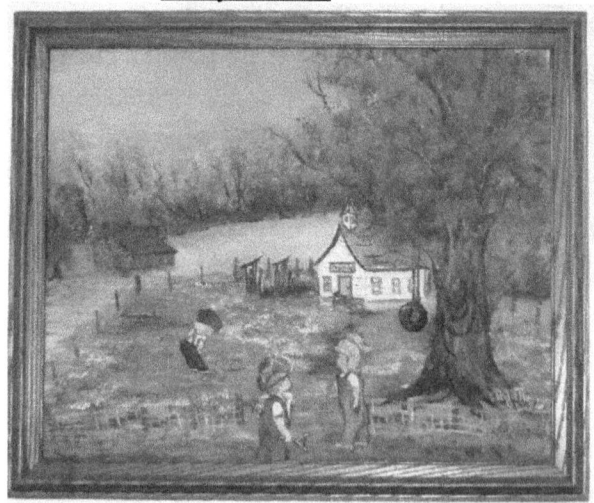

"Rules, Recess and Arithmetic" -oil painting
Original designer of the children unknown.

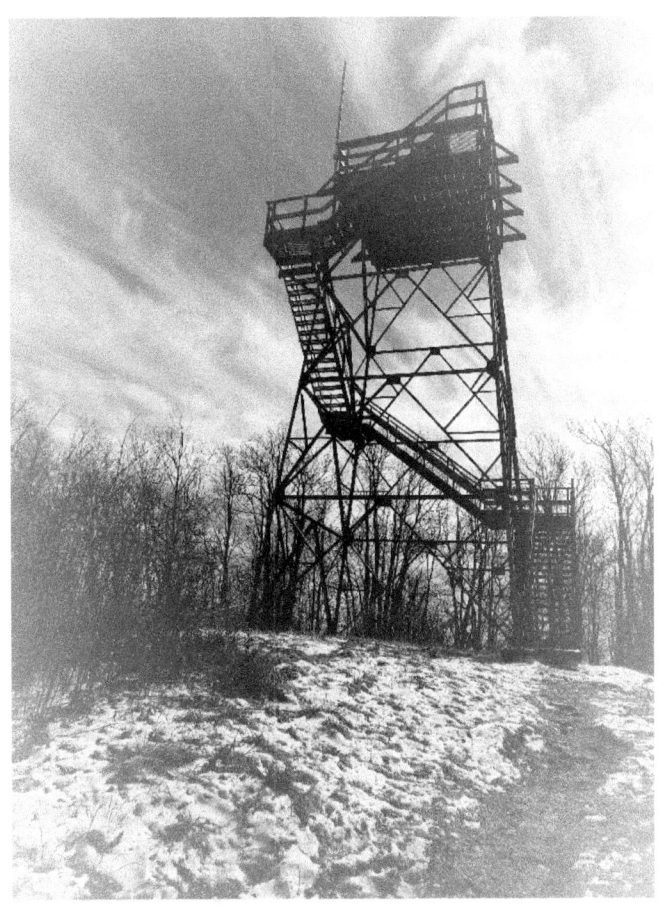

Psalms 18:2: "The LORD is my rock, and my fortress, and my deliverer; my God, my strength, in whom I will trust; my buckler, and the horn of my salvation, and my high tower."

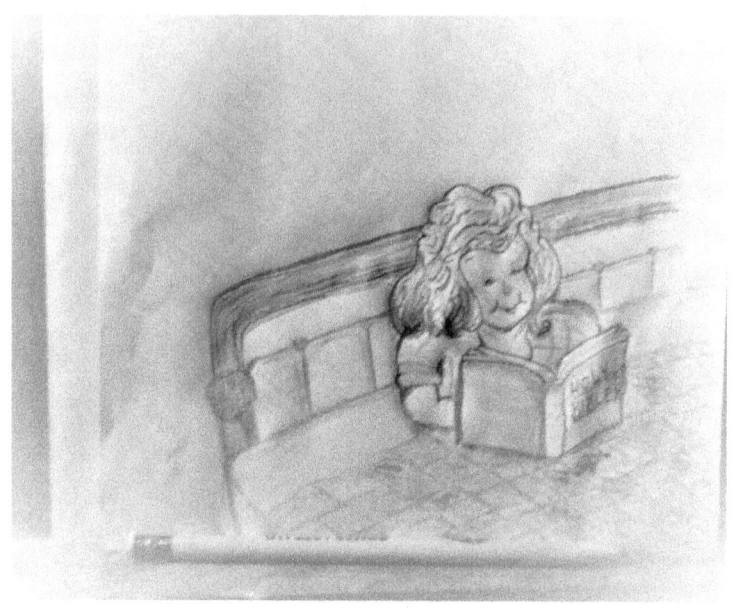

In this sketch, I added my iron bed, the Bible
and a quilt. The original scene was somewhat
different, original artist unknown. Most of my
art was created from a visual aid. Later in this
book and in Volume Two and Three you will
read how the Bible and quilts have become an
important part of my life.

VOLUME ONE

OVERCOMING LIFE'S

CHALLENGES...THROUGH CHRIST

Inspirational Thoughts, Valuable Lessons
Learned ...and still learning

~~~

"I've seen your sacrifices your blessings are
on the way!" Love, God

~~~

You know, these days we are always in a
rush. Seems there is no time to stop and think.
Life demands us to hurry here and hurry there,
with no rest for the weary...one day, we will
eventually be there... HOME... finally at rest...
forever! So, amidst the rushing, let's take a
breath, take in the beauty, cherish life... for
we're not There, yet!

~~~

Through Our Trials We Learn to Have Compassion...

II Corinthians 1:4 "Who comforteth us in all our tribulation, that we may be able to comfort them which are in trouble, by the comfort wherewith we ourselves are comforted of God."

Hebrews 3:13, 14 "But exhort one another daily, while it is called To-day; lest any of you be hardened through the deceitfulness of sin." 14. "For we are made partakers of Christ, if we hold the beginning of our confidence stedfast unto the end;"

Isaiah 50:4 "The Lord God hath given me the tongue of the learned, that I should know how to speak a word in season to him that is weary: he wakeneth morning by morning, he wakeneth mine ear to hear as the learned."

John 14:27 "Peace I leave with you, my peace I give to you; not as the world giveth, give I unto you. Let not your heart be troubled, neither let it be afraid."

Isaiah 41:10 "Fear thou not; for I am with thee: be not dismayed; for I am thy God: I will strengthen thee; yea, I will help thee; yea, I will uphold thee with the right hand of my righteousness.

~~~

Stay Focused

As you will read throughout this book there are many topics, I have shared that are common to us all. Many of these I have struggled with over the years and some I am still struggling with. We all fail and need God's grace to keep us on track. The most important key is to stay focused on Christ, with daily meditation on His word, being mindful of His voice, and being determined to make Heaven our home, our final resting place.

Are we purposing in our hearts to honor Him with our daily lives? I agree we are not perfect however we must strive for His perfect will, becoming more submissive and less rebellious. You may be strong in one area that I may be extremely weak in or vice versa. Sometimes, I think we get amnesia and/or anxiety, forgetting how we were carried during our lowest valleys. We may at times even be rattled with fear rather than be at peace having faith. Therefore, let's pray one for another, keep our priorities in line and Stay Focused!

~~~

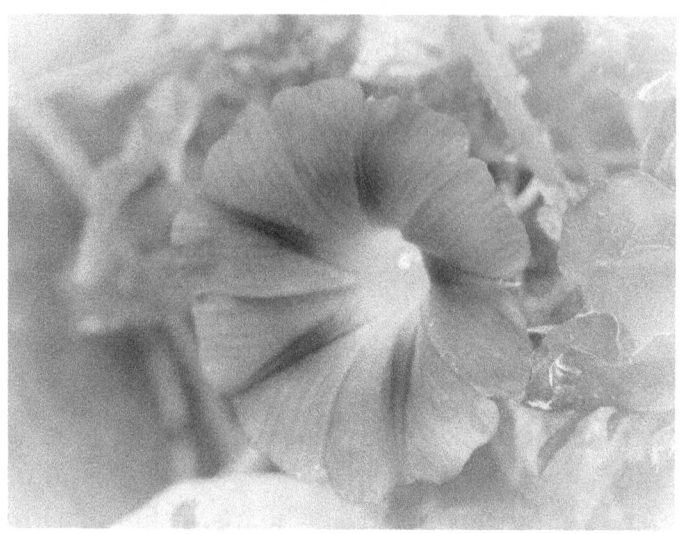

"Good Mornin'… Glory"
With each new day we are greeted with His
Glory, His mercy and His love!

~~~

We Are Not to Mirror the World but to Be a Reflection, of the SON!

Let me begin by telling you I am not a theologian or Bible scholar, I too am learning and seeking the Lord for understanding and wisdom. You will find many of the scriptures referenced in this book may be taken out of context. Therefore, I would encourage you to read the whole chapter from which the scriptures are taken and then read again the quoted passages. I have found when I clear the clutter from my life and purge myself of worldly desires, my heart and mind are more receptive.

Let's pray for wisdom as we learn together! We understand the definition of the words may not be as we think due to the Greek meanings... therefore we should study, do our homework! He tells us in II Timothy 2:15 to study to shew ourselves approved, rightly dividing the Word of God. We know we are saved by grace and are no longer under the law, John 10:28 tells us no man can pluck us out of His hand. I, however, believe willfully sinning can cause our name to be blotted out, read passages Hebrews 10:26 and Revelations 3:5. Why take that chance? In other words, His Grace does not give us permission to willfully sin. John 10:26 tells us if we are His sheep, we will hear His voice. I have found when I fast, during the fast, and the longer I fast, the more clearly, I could hear His voice. I have also been reprimanded when I got out of line which lets me know He does warn us when we are not staying close to the cross or being mindful of His will.

If society was studying or watching our lives as role models and if we were choosing to live our old lifestyles and yet continue to claim the title of Christian, then it would be quite difficult for them to depict what Christianity really means. What if we were the only Bible people read? What are we portraying to society? Commitment matters!!!! II Cor. 6:17 tells us to come out from among them and be ye a separate people. Do we think we need to live carelessly or haphazardly, or do we think we need to be a light for a dark world? Are we reflecting the SON? Are we seeking for a closer walk with the Lord or are we too busy?

John 4:23 tells us to worship Him in spirit and in truth. If we needed someone to intercede on our behalf, who would we choose? Someone who lives what they preach or someone who claims to be a Christian with no evidence? Of course, we would choose someone who reflects love and kindness, a fine example of Christ! Remember James 5:16 "Confess your faults, one to another, and pray for another, that ye may be healed. The effectual fervent prayer of a righteous man availeth much." We know in our hearts where we stand with the Lord! When the trumpet sounds will we be ready or will we hear the words depart from me, I never knew you found in Matthew 7:22,23?

Titus 2:12 pretty much sums this up, "Teaching us that, denying ungodliness and worldly lusts, we should live soberly, righteously and Godly, in this present world."

Also, in the book of Malachi we can find our responsibilities, concerning tithing. Verse 10: "Bring ye all the tithes into the storehouse, that there may be meat in mine house, and prove me now herewith, saith the Lord of hosts, if I will not open the windows of heaven, and pour you out a blessing, that there shall not be room enough to receive it." Why should we expect God to bless us if we aren't doing our part? I am not saying we are to work to earn our salvation! We know better than that! I have learned from experience we can NOT outgive God! As we mature in the Lord, we will desire to do His work. Then our reflections will be magnified and radiate even further. We are not to mirror the world, misleading society however we ARE, to be a reflection, of the SON guiding the world toward Him!

Ephesians 2:10; James 1:2,3,5,8,14,15,19-22,26; II Peter 2:21; II Peter 3:9,10; Galatians 1:10; James 4:17; II Timothy 2:16; Rev. 2:4,5; Rev. 3:5; Rev. 22:12,13; I Tim. 6:11, 21; Ephes. 6; Ephes. 4:26,27; James 5:16; II Cor. 13:5; II Cor. 12:20,21; Gal. 6:7-9; Gal. 5: 19-26; Gal. 5: 1; Matthew 7:21; Hebrews 10:26; I Peter 3:14; John 1:8-10; Hebrews 10:26

~~~

Thank You, Lord for reviving me with Your "CPR" (Comfort, Peace, Reassurance)

My late husband and I used to go mountain climbing as you will read in Volume Two. After his death it was as if a part of me had died. There was such an empty, indescribable feeling! I loved him since I was a teenager... my first love! When I rededicated my life to the Lord, I then realized what real love was...

When I was standing in the deepest pit of the valley, longing for that mountain top, searching effortlessly for the sight of the top of the ridge with betrayal and despair lingering, I could barely catch my breath! Oh, how the darkness within blinded my view! The brokenness I felt inside made that destination that he and I made so many times before now seem unfathomable.

Lord, as I heard Your still small voice whispering, beckoning me to trust You for guidance, I slowly began to identify that familiar voice I once knew. The people You strategically placed in my path allowed me to see Your presence, for that I am eternally grateful! Your reassurance that I am loved by You, accepted and wanted... I then began to comprehend a love unlike any other, what an epiphany! When I face adversity or become overwhelmed, You, gently remind me You are near… compelling me to trust Your exchange of peace for my shattered heart. Thank You for holding me when inside I felt not only my heart was in smithereens, but my world forever changed! Thank You for believing in me over and over even though I falter daily. There are not enough words for me to convey to You my gratitude for the love I feel from You! I think of the days no one saw my tears except You and oh how You knew my hurt, shame, grief, confusion, betrayal, emptiness, anxieties, and fears ...my failures! Then the peace that was manifested from You, calming my inner being for those times I know and believe in You, Jesus!!! In my deepest, darkest valleys You cradled me ever so gently! Thank You! Since my rededication, I think of the ridges You have helped me conquer and how we stood there together has helped me to grow stronger spiritually.

I know I have much more of learning to grasp, longing for Your word to be hidden within my heart! I thank You for the transformation thus far and Your willingness to repeatedly place me on the wheel, as a potter would do as if he was perfecting a piece of clay.

Also, I love You, Lord for caring about those who are dear to my heart and for patiently waiting for their return to You …Just as You waited for me!

I thank You for answering my prayers even when the answers were sometimes "No"! For I have learned You know what is best for me and through those times I have learned to trust Your guidance. Thank You for helping me to appreciate all things great and small. I have learned the difference of the things I once considered great which are now considered small and the things, I once considered small now are great. Thank You for teaching me I am no one's judge and to love all mankind-prestige or poor.

I pray I seize every chance to be a light to others, being mindful of their need for Your CPR. May my light illuminate, and not be dim! No matter what is happening in the lives of others help me to stay focused on Your plan for my life. Help me to shine, for Your glory! Help me to count each situation I encounter as a teaching tool or a learning experience. Thank You for extending grace and mercy to me, teaching me this is now my duty to extend to others. Thank You for walking beside me, leading and loving me. You are more than a

Higher Power! You are my best friend! YOU are my SAVIOR!

It is because of You, I can smile! It is because You gave me C.P.R I can live again!

Becoming a single mom sure sent my world upside down almost as though I died inside...Jesus truly revived me with his way of performing C.P.R.!!! ...More about that in Volume Two.

Romans 15:4 "For whatsoever things were written aforetime were written for our learning, that we through patience and comfort of the scriptures might have hope."

2Cor.4; 2 Cor.6:16-18; 1Peter 3:17; 2Cor. 6:4-7; Ephesians 5:17; Ephesians 6:11-17; 1John 5:14; Romans 2; Romans 3:1,2,10,11;

~~~

Do Good Unto Others

When people are placed in our paths, we must seek for guidance from the Lord on how to encourage them or help them in a way they will see Christ through us. Sometimes it is just being a confident friend with a listening ear that a person needs. They may not always be placed there, for a lengthy period of time, cherish each day together. There may come a time when they intentionally or unintentionally hurt us after we have tried to do everything possible to befriend them. Remember to search and pray for the Lord to reveal truth, wisdom, and if any forgiveness is needed, forgive! Let's not take it personal, for Christ was rejected and pushed away after all that He has done for us! Lest we forget, we MUST keep a guard on our mouths, for our reactions are valuable to our testimony!

Learning to let go is a hard lesson in life I agree, although we must appreciate the fact that there were times, we were chosen to set the standard by being an example of Christ. There was a reason for the acquaintance although we may hurt...again forgive them...and carry on doing the Lord's work. Time and again through my hurt I have heard that still small voice, say, to me "Don't let the hurt make you bitter", OH MY, how that rumbled through my mind, and humbled my heart!

I can recall times I thought I had finally found that special someone who I had been waiting for. I began to remove the bricks one at a time slowly lowering the wall little by little that I had built around my heart only to find out later I was needing more cement and plenty more cinderblocks to rebuild it. Over the last few years I have been more careful about starting relationships, I admit there were times, I was fearful of rejection. I have learned to proceed slowly, being more mindful, to pray for direction. I may have even pushed people away due to trust issues.

When we are in the early stages of relationships we must keep in mind what our goals are: Do we want to be in a relationship due to that person's high paying job, due to that person's outward beauty or do we want to be in a relationship we will be happy in years later when the looks are gone and the bank account is low? Is that person a Christian? Does he or she have the same beliefs as we do? These are important questions that will affect the relationship down the road. It may take some time to recognize the red flags so we must keep our standards high, our minds on Christ and if the other person who we thought was going to be our knight in shining armor loses his luster, we can be satisfied knowing we were an example of a true Christian.

Can we think of a time we hurt someone? Were we humble enough to apologize? I think we all can answer yes to the first question, but how about the second question? I have seen people carry grudges for years! Let's not be overweight carrying bitterness, bodily weight is heavy enough! I admit, I too have hurt people and carried grudges! SHEW WEE, how good it felt when I turned those grudges over to God, felt like a heavy weight was lifted from me. Life was so much better once I let go!!!

I can think of a time when I carried a grudge for quite a while. Then one day on the banks of the river as we were awaiting a baptism, I realized the lady I was not very fond of was standing not far from me. As I looked across the river, I saw the cliffs and heard this scripture from Luke 19:40: If you don't praise Me, I will call for the rocks and hills to praise Me (paraphrased). It was then I knew in my heart I couldn't truly praise our Lord until I asked that person to forgive me for what I had said. No matter what she had done I had to do my part and when I did, I wasn't only able to praise Him, but I felt a ton of bricks lift from me.

1 Thessalonians 5: 14, 15 "Now we exhort you, brethren, warn them that are unruly, comfort the feebleminded, support the weak, be patient toward all men. 15 See that none render evil for evil unto any man; but ever follow that which is good, both among yourselves, and to all men. "Matthew 5:16, 44 "Let your light so shine before men, that they may see your good works, and glorify your Father which is in Heaven. But I say unto you, Love your enemies, bless them

that curse you, do good to them that hate you, and pray for them which despitefully use you, and persecute you."

Matthew 7:12 "Therefore all things whatsoever ye would that man should do to you, do ye even so to them..."

~~~

Does This One Go to the Landfill or Recycle Bin?

Awhile back I was driving through a city and glanced over to a garbage truck that was just ahead of me in the other lane. On the back of that truck was a large teddy bear hanging over the back bar of the truck. I was thinking how cute that was and what a neat idea to make people smile then after I got a closer look, I discovered the bear was torn then I felt saddened. I began thinking at one time that bear may have been a child's playmate. Of course, my mind began to wonder and pondered the what if's. What if someone would have loved him with his differences he would not be where he was today? What if someone would have sewn him and taught a child to appreciate his differences? This story reminded me of the potter and the clay. Aren't you glad God didn't throw the clay away when we were on the potter's wheel? How many times has He sewn us up, remolded us or reshaped us from the strong winds of the stormy sea of life? I give Him praise today for not only renewing my mind daily but for the way He loves me! He loves me not only gently, but profoundly enough to discipline me when I am wrong. This story also reminds me of the song "The Broken Ones" by Talley Trio, referring to repairing those who have been shattered from life's storms.

Jeremiah 18:1-6 "The word which came to Jeremiah from the Lord, saying, 2. Arise, and go down to the potter's house, and there I will cause thee to hear my words. 3. Then I went down to the potter's house, and, behold, he wrought a work on the wheels. 4. And the vessel that he made of clay was marred in the hand of the potter: So, he made it again another vessel, as seemed good to the potter to make it. 5. Then the word of the Lord came to me, saying, 6. O house of Israel, cannot I do with you as this potter? saith the Lord. Behold, as the clay is in the potter's hand, so are ye in mine hand, O house of Israel."

~~~

Trust... Fear... Respect

Later, you will read where my favorite cat sat in the recliner with me as I was studying and writing. Well, that same beloved feline that I became so attached to, later required me to have stitches in my lip! Still not sure why he attacked me but to my surprise one evening while I was removing him from my desk he turned unexpectedly and bit my lip repeatedly, refusing to stop! I suppose when I got scared and tried to get him to let go, he went into fight mode and became even more fierce! That was quite an ordeal to say the least! I cried for several days from the shock and the betrayal I felt. I remember as the doctor was stitching the wound closed, she commented how I would most likely have a scar. I said, at this age and point in my life if someone could not look past a scar then they must not be a true friend anyway. The thought then came to me, those we love who we thought were our friends can leave inner scars, and animals we love, and thought were our best buddies can leave outer scars. However, Jesus is One who looks past our scars and would never betray us, a true Friend indeed! Do you know Him as friend? If so, do you share with others the kind of friend He is?

I felt like I was being tortured when I was told I had to keep the cat for ten days and continue to take care of him. I did not want to look at him let alone care for him! During those ten days I learned no matter if we have physical pain or emotional pain, we are not to let the hurt make us bitter! The next evening after the incident one of our other cats came to me and put her paws up on my legs and I cringed and cried. Just the thought of a cat getting near me was so upsetting and I have always been a cat lover. Yes, they can be aggravating at times but can also be very therapeutic. The feelings of great sadness overwhelmed me thinking I would never be able to bond like that again with a cat because of this incident.

Then, I found myself feeling sorry for the cat. He is so skittish towards everyone else, I wondered what would happen to him if I gave him away? I also learned they surely can be temperamental at times. One of the outdoor cats had gotten inside as we were leaving. He and Sabby do not get along so I am sure Sab was a bit rattled by the time we returned that evening. He was also behind on his flea medicine so evidently my face/lip was in the wrong place at the wrong time, possibly mistaken as a flea. I am no longer paralyzed by fear when a cat gets near me. Now, I can pet him or her but have learned the difference between fear and respect, my space and their space.

~~~

Let's Do a Soul Check

Here are some questions to help us stay focused and as someone would use spell check on the computer, these are for us to do a soul check.

Am I ready if I should die right now? Am I on fire for God, or am I lukewarm? Have I been praying fervently for the lost and the prayer requests? Have I been showing compassion and not just feeling compassionate? When was the last time I was in my prayer closet? How much time do I spend humbly, down on my knees? Throughout the day do I seek the Lord, not only seeking Him, but listening attentively to Him? Am I living with discouragement and expecting answers from God when I am not using my time communicating with him? When I fasted, did I hold up to my end of the fasting? Do I begin my day with prayer? What are some idols that have hindered my time with God? Am I the example I would like to see in others?

Jude 22: "And of some *have compassion, making a difference*"

41

Rev. 2:5 "Remember therefore from whence thou art fallen, *and repent, and do the first works*; or else I will come unto thee quickly, and will remove thy candlestick out of his place, except thou repent."

Rev. 2:10 "Fear none of those things which thou shalt suffer: behold, the devil shall cast some of you into prison, that ye may be tried; and ye shall have tribulation ten days: be thou faithful unto death, and *I will give thee a crown of life.*"

Rev. 3:5 "*He that over-cometh,* the same shall be clothed in white raiment; and I will not blot out his name out of the book of life, but I will confess his name before my Father, and before his angels."

Rev. 3:15, 16 "*I know thy works, thou art neither cold nor hot*: I would thou wert cold or hot. 16 So then because thou art lukewarm, and neither cold, not hot, I will spue thee out of my mouth."

Rev 8:17 "For the Lamb which is in the midst of the throne shall feed them, and shall lead them unto living fountains of waters: and *God shall wipe away all tears from their eyes*."

Rev 14:13 "And I heard a voice from heaven saying unto me, Write, Blessed are the dead which die in the Lord from henceforth: Yea, saith the Spirit, that *they may rest from their labours*; and their works do follow them."

Now, let's go back and read what is in italics. Yes, they are taken out of context but think about each one and be encouraged today!

~~~

Strength for the Hurdles of Life

By now you are probably thinking who am, I, to tell you how to live a Godly life, and you are exactly right! I am not exempt from the temptations and snares of this life, I fail and am ashamed, my faith gets low and I struggle with battles that are common to us all. I could not tell you of the times I had to go back and read parts of this book to be able to jump hurdles like forgiveness and bitterness. The scriptures referenced here do not dissipate over time! His Word renews us, restores our faith, and gives us wisdom to make the right choices. We all have hurdles to jump in this journey called life. Keep Jumping!

Last night as I was needing strength from the Lord, I began reading His word and once again was amazed at how He knew where I needed to read and what I was feeling. Here are some scriptures He revealed to me, hope they bless you as much as they have me: Matthew 15:28

"Jesus said, "O woman, great is thy faith: be it unto thee even as thou will." How awesome it would be to hear those words from Jesus! I must admit my faith gets weak from time to time and to hear him say, "N..., great is thy faith" It not only gives me chills but humbles me as I subconsciously hit the repeat button. We can choose to doubt, or we can choose to believe. It is that simple! Matthew 17: 20, 21: Jesus said, "Because of your unbelief; for verily I say unto you, If ye have faith as a grain of mustard seed, ye shall say unto this mountain, Remove thee hence to yonder place; and it shall remove; and nothing shall be impossible to you." The next verse is the one I need to do more of. Verse 21 "Howbeit this kind goeth not out but by prayer and fasting." II Timothy 2:15 tells us to study, I believe we will be accountable for what we have or have not done. It is up to us to study and seek God's guidance, He never ceases to amaze me when I apply the effort. Romans 8:25 "But if we hope for that we see not, then do we with patience wait for it." I must admit I am very impatient at times. Isaiah 46:4 "And even to your old age, I am he, and even to hoar hairs will I carry you; I have made, and I will bear, even I will carry and will deliver you." I love this! That scripture goes right along with Psalms 37:25 "I have been young, and now am old; yet have I not seen the righteous forsaken, nor his seed begging bread." Psalms 55:22 "Cast thy burden upon the Lord, and he shall sustain thee: he shall never suffer the righteous to be moved." When we wholeheartedly trust Him, He is faithful and has proved time and again He will provide for us. II Timothy 2:16 "But shun profane and vain babblings: for they will increase unto more ungodliness." Matthew 12:36 "But I say unto you, That every idle word that men shall speak" (that includes women too), "they shall give account thereof in the day of judgement". Verse 37: "For by thy words thou shalt be justified, and by thy words thou shalt be condemned." II Timothy 3:4 "...lovers of pleasure more than lovers of God;" How many times do we choose to do other things rather than study, pray or reach out to others? II Timothy 3:5 "Having a form of Godliness but denying the power thereof..." May we never be ashamed to worship! He also tells us to not quench the spirit in I Thessalonians 5:19. Matthew 12:25 "And Jesus knew their thoughts..." He knows us and loves us unconditionally. We all fail but we must keep striving for we know He is truly the best friend that has stood by us through our darkest valleys as well as our highest peaks. May you be encouraged, today!

~~~

Self -Discipline, Are We There Yet?

I must admit I have made some bad choices and am not alone in seeing the results. I have chosen to indulge in unhealthy foods especially late at night when I am relaxing. Last night, Curt (my adult son, who is nonverbal) drew a picture of me, which made me realize what others perceive as they look at me. Yes, I am ashamed, I can't seem to win this battle of weight loss on my own. I attribute my weight gain to stress. In, reality, it is due to not having self-discipline! When one lacks in self-discipline/control he or she allows addictions to become priorities. My health suffers along with time devoted to studying God's word. It is so easy to grab some chocolate and a glass of milk or a tasty snack, kick back and relax. It takes some effort to apply our minds to reading, thinking, meditating, and listening for direction. Fasting and gluttony are two areas I need to concentrate more on, how about you?

Some days I feel overwhelmed with daily tasks. I shut down and do not get things accomplished that are needful and do other things, some which are important and some which are not. Quilt making is enjoyable and part of my ministry but devoting too much time in my sewing room there again can display lack of self-discipline.

I remember on my grade cards from elementary school there was a box sometimes checked, makes wise use of time. The older I get the more this statement comes to my mind, if I was to get a grade card from God would that box be checked? Am I devoting too much time on unnecessary tasks? One thing I have learned, time is very valuable, why not share some rather than waste it? There are so many people who are broken, hurt, in need of love, and in need of our time!!!! How much of our time do we give away? How much time do we waste?

I rededicated my life to the Lord on July 10, 2011. My relationship with Christ is more personal now than it was years ago, much more intimate! My outlook on life has changed quite a bit since I rededicated my life to Him. Maybe by being a widow, I now realize how much more I rely on Him and the importance of self-discipline. No! I am not there, yet! What are some of your struggles, lessons or experiences?

Matthew 6:16-18 "Moreover when ye fast, be not, as the hypocrites, of a sad countenance:

for they disfigure their faces, that they may appear unto men to fast. Verily I say unto you, They have their reward. 17. But thou, when thou fastest, anoint thine head, and wash thy face; 18. That thou appear not unto men to fast, but unto thy Father which is in secret: and thy Father, which seeth in secret, shall reward thee openly."

Philippians 4:13, "I can do all things through Christ which strengtheneth me."

1 Corinthians 3:13-16 13. "Every man's work shall be made manifest: for the day shall declare it, because it shall be revealed by fire; and the fire shall try every man's work of what sort it is. 14. If any man's work abide which he hath built thereupon, he shall receive a reward. 15. If any man's work shall be burned, he shall suffer loss; but he himself shall be saved; yet so as by fire. 16. Know ye not that ye are the temple of God, and that the spirit of God dwelleth in you."

1 Corinthians 4:1 "Let a man so account of us, as of the ministers of Christ, and stewards of the mysteries of God."

~~~

Admitting is the First Step of Identifying Addiction

To be overcomers, we must admit our addictions! You have read where unhealthy snacks were one, a difficult battle indeed, now another one I admit was social media! God had spoken to me on several occasions how that was an idol in my life, and we all know how God feels about idols. Even though I hated to admit it, He was right! I would turn on the computer first thing in the morning and check back throughout the day, sometimes sitting in front of the computer for hours. I would tell myself this was okay due to loneliness.

Excuses are easily made when we are addicted! Admitting my addiction was the first step, making changes was step two. I had to pray hard, for many times I tried on my own then I would revert right back. Addictions are a daily struggle! I can't imagine how someone addicted to drugs must feel.

The conviction I felt had me turning the computer off and spending time studying, working, praying, devoting more time meditating on God, and spending time with family. I soon learned how the computer had become an idol in my life. I grew closer to God, felt his presence even more, and loved that feeling. Therefore, understood more in depth why He was convicting me.

I do check social media, send and answer messages, and pray over the prayer requests. I do like talking to my family and friends, especially those I have not seen in a while. I enjoy viewing their photos; however, I must keep God first in my life and limit my time on there. I have found when I was on social media a lot, I became depressed. When I stopped being so engrossed in all the posts, I learned to pray and leave them in God's hands. This choice made a positive change in my life. I wonder what the outcome will be in our children's lives if we do not limit their time on social media or technology in general?

Think of how much time we could give to His work and our families if we transform those hours on social media to cooking for someone, visiting, or making a gift for someone. Our homes would be a lot cleaner and our testimonies would be more powerful, and relationships would be happier. I am sure you notice as well as I, everyone is on a cell phone, now days! We see people staring into a phone and some even have them attached to their ear. We see them in doctors' offices, while driving and even while shopping. People are so engrossed with technology whether it's a social media site or a way to communicate! What if we all were that in tune with God? What a transformation we could make!

I Cor. 10:14 "Wherefore, my dearly beloved, flee from idoltry."

I John 5:21 "Little children keep yourselves from idols."
II Kings 17:12 "For they served idols, whereof the Lord had said unto them, Ye shall not do this thing."

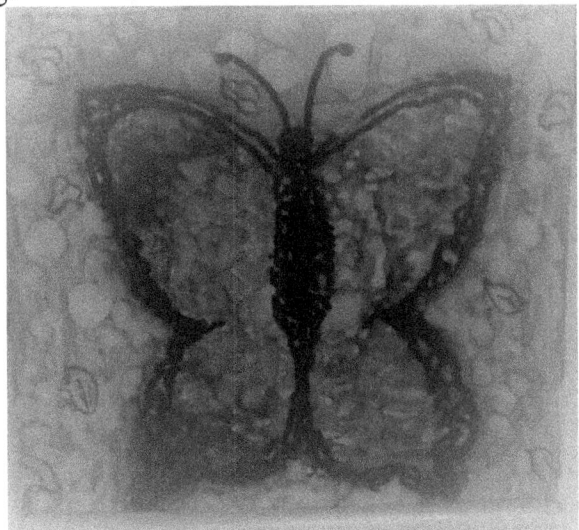

"The Transformation" …medium: metallic-alcohol ink

~~~

Expectations Misunderstood

Occasionally, expectations of others are not always the expectations of God! Our bodies need rest and care as well as our spiritual man needs fed! Feeling deflated and stressed reduces intimate time with Jesus! We all have a ministry, a calling on our lives yet how would we be able to minister if we are starved? Yes, we do need to help others by first seeking guidance. Not to be busy to the point that we do not take time to study and pray.

Moreover, I do believe we are to come together in unity. The scripture Hebrews 10:25 tells us to not forsake the assembling of ourselves together, exhorting one another, the more we see that day approaching. We are to come together to worship and give Him well deserved Praise! Our work or ministry can be inside the church such as teaching, preaching or singing, as well as other jobs. However, I believe our biggest ministry is outside the Church! We are to work not only to shew forth our faith, but because we love the Lord. Our joy should be evident and splattering onto others as we pass by!

What is your ministry? If everyone was a teacher who would visit the sick? If everyone was quilt maker who would feed the hungry? If everyone was a prayer warrior who would encourage the young mother or uplift the young man who is becoming a father? Yes, we can do several of these jobs but let us be mindful and seek guidance as to what God expects of us. Some may not be able to go, yet we can pray for those who do go. He knows our capabilities and our heart's desire. There are different situations or circumstances beyond one's control that may hinder us from working the fields. He also knows our excuses or laziness. He tells us not to be slothful! When we whole heartedly seek Him for guidance, He knows what we are capable of and will not put more on us than we can bear. In Volume Two, you will read what my life is like being a mother of a child with differing abilities and sometimes how my plans had to be changed. We, (my son and I) recently have found a ministry we can do together and oh how I love that feeling of fulfillment at the end of the day!

Acts 5:29 "Then Peter and the other apostles answered and said, We ought to obey God rather than men."

Matthew 9:37 "...The harvest truly is plenteous, but the labourers are few;"
I Peter 4:11-16; I Cor. 2:5; Gal. 6:10; Phil. 4:6-9; James 1:22; James 2:18, 26; Peter 1:7; Proverbs 19:24

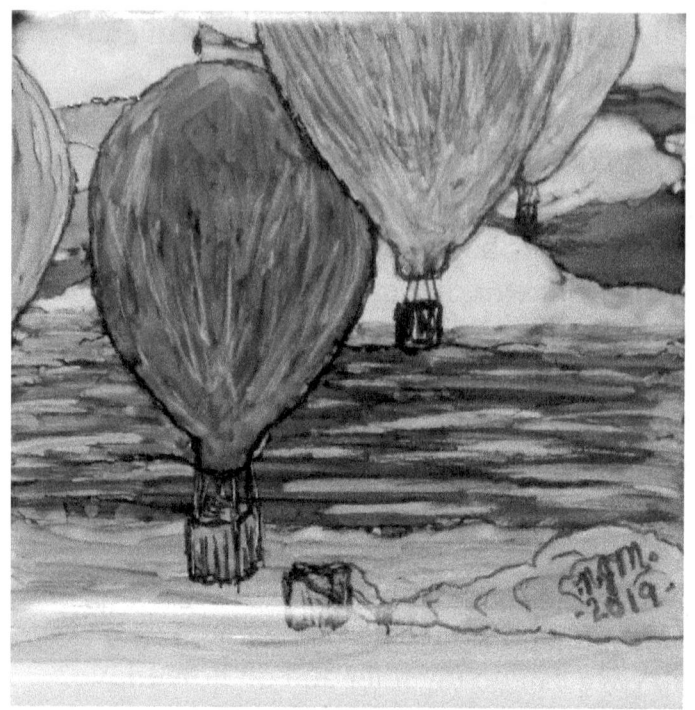

"Which one are you, spiritually?" …alcohol ink

~~~~

Admitting My Fears

We all have faults and being able to admit them is the beginning of correcting them. Being the baby of the family, I have a fear that is difficult to explain and until now I have not really tried. Just recently I guess the fear has appeared more through the lens of my emotions. I was sheltered and protected as a child, then went from home into marriage so never experienced independence as someone for example who went off to college. After Saul's death (my late husband), and our oldest two children (Josh and Olivia) had moved out, Curt (my youngest son) and I did not live here very long until my sister moved in. Prior to her moving in was the only time I felt independent. To my surprise, I slept well at night. Now that sis' cancer level continues to rise despite the treatments, and that my parents aren't getting any younger, I feel a form of fear of being alone. I fear there will be no one physically to protect me and mentally to support me.

Maybe this is what anxiety feels like, which brings me to a scripture in the Bible, Philippians 4:6 "Be careful for nothing; but in every thing by prayer and supplication with thanksgiving let your requests be made known unto God." Also, the scripture in Philippians 4:11 tells us "Not that I speak in respect of want: for I have learned, in whatsoever state I am, there with to be content". Therefore, I am learning to exchange fears for trust.

Proverbs 3:24 - "When thou liest down, thou shalt not be afraid: yea, thou shalt lie down, and thy sleep shall be sweet."

Psalms 4:8 - "I will both lay me down in peace, and sleep: for thou, Lord, only makest me dwell in safety."

Isaiah 41:13 "For I the Lord thy God will hold thy right hand, saying unto thee, Fear not: I will help thee."

Matthew 8:26 "And he saith unto them, Why are ye fearful, O ye of little faith? Then he arose, and rebuked the winds and the sea; and there was a great calm."

Romans 8:15,18,25,31,37-39 15."For ye have not received the spirit of bondage again to fear; but ye have received the Spirit of adoption, whereby we cry, Abba, Father." 18."For I reckon that the sufferings of this present time are not worthy to be compared with the glory which shall be revealed in us." 25. "But if we hope for that we see not, then do we with patience wait for it." 31. "What shall we then say to these things? If God be for us, who can be against us?" 37. "Nay, in all these things we are more than conquerors through Him that loved us." 38. "For I am persuaded, that neither death, nor life, nor angels, nor principalities, not powers, nor things present, nor things to come," 39. "Nor height, nor depth, nor any other creature, shall be able to separate us from the love of God, which is in Christ Jesus our Lord."

~~~

Overcoming My Fears

Needless, to say, the final copy was not printed before my original deadline therefore I am able to share with you an experience I had on the morning of New Year's Eve. I was scheduled to do pre-op on Dec. 30. During that time the response to one of the pre-op questions was puzzling to the nurse and amazing to myself. She asked, "who would be with you during the surgery"? I was scheduled to have a complete hysterectomy the next morning. I replied, No one. She said, "You know you cannot drive yourself home so who will be there"? I said, I understand that, however I will be able to drive myself to the hospital then explained my situation of my sister battling cancer, my son who has differing abilities and my parents are not as healthy as they used to be, therefore I am trusting God.

She had no clue what I had previously written in this book about fearing things especially the unknown. God has enabled me to place my fears in Him, for His track record is incomparable! I did not want my family or friends to have to sit in the waiting room for hours and besides, they could only go so far but

I knew having Jesus with me, He would stay with me through it all. He could go through the operating room doors, guide the doctor's hands and comfort me through the recovery. I had to prove to myself that YES, "I can do ALL things through CHRIST who strengthens me"! (Remember that scripture?) Therefore, I did not tell many people I was going to have surgery. Later, I did have visitors, family and friends came by which meant a lot to me! I was also surprised to see my daughter who came home from college to spend the night at the hospital with me which was more comforting than she will ever know. Today makes a week since the surgery and I have never once had to complain about being hungry or wonder who would be here to care for sis or Curt. God always makes a way and this time was no different.

Hebrews 13:5: "Let your conversation be without covetousness; and be content with such things as ye have; for he hath said, I will never leave thee, nor forsake thee."

Joshua 1:5,7: "There shall not any man be able to stand before thee all the days of thy life: as I was with Moses, so I will be with thee: I will not fail thee, nor forsake thee." 7. "Only be thou strong and very courageous..."

Jeremiah 1:5: "Before I formed thee in the belly, I knew thee; before thou camest forth out of the womb I sanctified thee...."

~~~

Don't Let the Hurt Make You Bitter

After writing this diary entry (which later became a narrative in Volume Three), I felt very strongly this title was to be the title of this book. (Although there are now Volumes One, Two and Three.) Many times, my sister and I would refer to this title, reminding each other to not let the hurt one of us was feeling at that moment, make us bitter.

I have been having a "woe is me" the last few days. I was reluctant to post updates on a social media site due to how people react, compared to how they actually show their love and support. Things such as taking the time to visit my sister, who is battling this horrific epidemic called cancer. She has been back home now for over a year. I was thinking of all the days we have been here and rarely see any new faces in the house. Her surgery was in June 2014 and she was finally able to come home in October, of that year. The road ahead was uncertain, not quite the way I imagined our lives to be.

Some of those days she was greeted with visitors, but it seems as the days passed, the time between visits have broadened. God spoke to me about becoming bitter. These are the words I clearly heard, "Don't let the hurt make you bitter!" I have had to ask Him to help me because within myself I had become bitter.

Rather than allowing that bitterness to consume me, I will use this as a stepping stone and do my best to reach out to others who are hurting. I had learned that lesson before, but God knew I needed to hear this title... Oh, His timing!!! As I got the pen and paper out and began writing, Curt got the Bible from the coffee table and handed it to me and held up three fingers. (During the editing process I was in awe when I read that last sentence. I didn't know this book was going to take three years to write and that it would end up being three separate books.) Curt may not communicate verbally but most definitely he knew what I needed, "the Bible"!

I do get frustrated and the flesh side of me wants to withdraw, then I think how Jesus would expect me to react. I think of something I felt the Holy Spirit spoke to me recently, "How you react through all of this is your testimony and you never know who is watching to see your reactions through the rocky roads as well as the paved ones". I dropped my head in shame, changed my attitude and began to think upon His goodness.

It was then my style of writing journal entries changed. I have learned it is vital to not only have compassion, but to show compassion by loving on people. That is how people see Christ through us! Remember the scripture in Jude 22..."And of some have compassion, making a difference."

~~~

Becoming Godly Women

Now is not the time to be fearful but be confident, strong and bold! Study...Pray...Fast...Reach Out...Encourage! We must be brave and not back down as the fiery darts come!

Ladies, where are those prayer closets? Are we Godly women, united, as one, praying for one another? What about those prayer lists and scriptures that encourage us to keep strong in our endeavor? Think about the prayers that were answered when we fasted and prayed! Are we devoting our time to doing our duty as Christian women? May we always be about the Lord's work uplifting our sisters and brothers in Christ! We all have failed in some form or fashion however we are our sisters' and brothers' keeper. We should be hovering over them in prayer and not only offering a helping hand but asking and allowing God to show us how we can reach out to one another. Have we developed a bond with our sisters based on trust, love, support and friendship? Surely, if we tend to stay in the clique, we realize He wants us to step out of the clique and reach out to all, of our siblings in Christ and especially those who aren't saved.

Ephesians 6:12 "For we wrestle not against flesh and blood, but against principalities, against powers, against the rulers of darkness of this world, against spiritual wickedness in high places."

Ephesians 5:4,16,19 "Neither filthiness, nor foolish talking, nor jesting, which are not convenient: but rather giving of thanks. 16. Redeeming the time, because the days are evil. 19. Speaking to yourselves in psalms and hymns and spiritual songs, singing and making melody in your heart to the Lord."

Ephesians 4:29 "For no man ever yet hated his own flesh; but nourisheth and cherisheth it, even as the Lord the church:"

Titus 2:2-5 "That the aged men be sober, grave, temperate, sound in faith, in charity, in patience, 3. The aged women likewise, that they be in behavior as becometh holiness, not false accusers, not given to much wine, teachers of good things, 4. That they may teach the young women to be sober, to love their husbands, to love their children. 5. To be discreet, chaste, keepers at home, good, obedient to their own husbands, that the word of the God be not blasphemed.

Proverbs 27:2 "Let another man praise thee, and not thine own mouth; a stranger, and not thine own lips."

Proverbs 31 teaches us how to be virtuous women. However, I am only referencing a few verses of that chapter. 12. "She will do him good and not evil all the days of her life." 20. "She stretcheth out her hand to the poor; yea, she reacheth forth her hands to the needy." 27. "She looketh well to the ways of her household, and eateth not the bread of idleness." 30. "Favour is deceitful, and beauty is vain: but a woman that feareth the Lord, she shall be praised."

Galatians 6:10 "As we have therefore opportunity, let us do good unto all men, especially unto them who are of the household of faith."

Titus 3:2, 5, 9; Matthew 6:6; I Timothy 2:10, 5:10; Romans 14:16; I Cor. 10:13; Proverbs 28:27; Matt. 25:35; II Cor. 4:8, 9, 16-18; I John

3:14; Hebrews 11:6; Hebrews 13:6; I Tim. 2:10;
II Cor. 6:3-6; I Thes. 5:22; II Thes. 3:13; Col.
4:23; 1 John 4:20; 1 John 2:15-17;

~~~

With Age Comes Wisdom

* Kindness is a gift not only to the receiver but
to the giver as well.
* It's not the beauty you see in the mirror nor is
it in the glitter and glitz. What others see from
our hearts is what makes us shine!
* It is not the volume of the voice when
gossiping, that is irrelevant! It is the intent to
belittle others that speaks loudly.
* In the Bible, Joseph was betrayed by his
blood-line yet he forgave...grudges are time
wasted!
* Backbone is not just a body part!
* We must identify the source if we want to be
freed from loneliness, sadness, or any negative
thoughts.
* Do not let the conniving tactics of the devil
steal your song or your joy...Sing Louder!
* If you think you have nothing valuable to
give...the gift of your time is priceless!
* We all have a unique way of blessing
others...May we never forget the importance of
that!

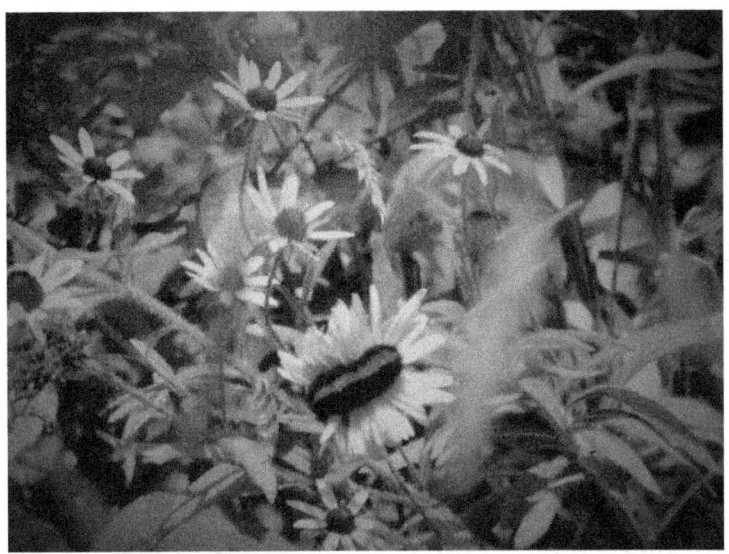

"Our uniqueness is His handiwork"
Remember the Bible verse, "Be still and know I am God"? Our uniqueness is important to His plan.

~~~

Let's Reflect

Let's stop for a minute and reflect...let's think back to the time when we were younger. Now think of the person or the people who impacted our lives in such a powerful way we never forgot them. Are we setting that kind of example for others?

As I look back there are several people who come to my mind, but I want to share with you only one of them. Did you grow up, subconsciously wanting to be like them? Now that you have that person or people in mind, ask yourself are your traits and their traits similar?

Now, I want to tell you of a lady who impacted my life. As a child, I could not help but over hear the adults' conversations. Their compliments or positive words spoke of how this compassionate woman would take food to people who were less fortunate, or by helping those going through a rough time. She showed compassion unselfishly, making a difference. She probably never knew how others were watching or how a little child like myself was impacted.

After I became an adult, I saw first-hand how she was still showing compassion and loving on people with a Godly love. There was a time period when her elderly mother needed care and she cared for her in her home. Later when she became unable, due to her own health condition to care for her in her own home, she went daily or almost daily taking food to her mother and sat by her mother's bedside along with some of her other siblings. I am sure there were more family who came to visit, during the times I wasn't there.

Her brother was often found there making sure his mother had fresh cold water as well.

They both had families of their own, but love led them back to check on their momma. They never knew or expected their devotion would one day be written in a book. The sights of them sitting by her bed faithfully was a testimony in and of itself.

After their mother's passing, this lady and her sister began volunteering helping other families as they endured the end of life stage with their loved ones. (You will read more about her sister, P.W. in Volume Three.) A few years ago, when I visited this lady's home, I learned our home decor was alike and we even have similar hobbies. She also had made some of the most beautiful detailed quilts and paintings. No matter the challenges/hurt that she or her family have faced over the years, they did not let the hurt make them bitter! She (L.T.), her siblings, and their family have impacted many lives by their unfeigned love for others.

~~~

You Can't Max Out Your Blessings

I am at a point in my life where it seems that I am busy all the time! I never realized when I left my full-time job as a preschool teacher I would have so many things to get done. Some of which are opportunities for God to work through me and some are the jobs which would require both parents, if that were the case. Being a single mom, it seems I have double the workload.

As I age, I am learning this is a time where the little things mean the most and where memories are being made. Above it all, just how much I rely on God! One of the most cherished blessings is to be able to enjoy quality time with family and friends. A blessing that makes my heart leap with laughter!

We all seem to have an endless work load these days, but my gracious, how humbling we feel when God uses someone like us to do his work! It brings peace to our soul and a good night's rest, don't you agree? I heard a preacher once say, "We do not have to be able just, available. The Lord will equip us and make us able if we are willing to work." There were times deep inside I felt I was at the center of His will and there were times I know I could have applied more effort to whatever He was asking of me.

I still find it still amazing, when I see the evidence of God in the midst, as if a silent listener was nearby, as I was thinking aloud or to myself desiring this or that. Even though I do not deserve that kind of love He still blesses me!

I could not tell you of the times I would just be thinking of something we needed or sometimes I just wanted, then I would find whatever it was at a yard sale, thrift store, or given to me without that person hearing me say I was wanting or needing it. I even received discounts that weren't advertised, while shopping. There were times, I would come home to loads of wood in our yard during the winter months, or our yard mowed in the summer months. When our children were little there would be bags of nice clothing sent our way. I could walk you through our home and point out item after item how God blessed us in that way! I know God doesn't have favorites but sometimes I feel like I am one of his favorites.

In fact, one night I was wishing I could start going to the gym since the winter weather makes it somewhat impossible to be dedicated to the walking trail. I knew financially I could not afford the monthly fee due to the desperate need for home renovations. Then I turned on the news which I rarely watch and there he was, the fitness center owner, offering free memberships for a limited time. To qualify, one had to meet the criteria (exceed a certain weight, pass the interview and be willing to change eating habits). It was as if God once again sent me the solution when I thought the idea was impossible. I went for the interview (which I later, referred to, "as a pep talk from a stranger") and never did the question arise about my income. The director and his wife have a desire to help people become healthier due to their family history. I got so excited about a much-needed change in my life I wrote "Nanna is off to the gym". This felt like a Christmas present from God!

We can't max out our blessings! However, we are not to be boastful about the way God uses us to bless others, we are to direct all honor to Him! I think of the scriptures in Matthew 6:1-4 "Take heed that ye do not your alms before men, to be seen of them: otherwise ye have no reward of your Father which in in heaven. Therefore, when thou doest thine alms, do not sound a trumpet before thee, as the hypocrites do in the synagogues and in the streets, that they may have glory of men: Verily I say unto you, They have their reward. But when thou doest alms, let not thy left hand know what thy right hand doeth: That thine alms may be in secret: and thy Father which seeth in secret himself shall reward thee openly." I admit I have been like the hypocrite at times. I pray for God to help me to do His work without boasting! I am determined, to become more humble like those who have set examples before me.

One day, I was talking to God, wondering why things seem to remain the same, having myself a pity party. He then He reminded me He hasn't stopped blessing me then I heard, "You can't max out your blessings!"

Never be afraid to give! Do you remember the story in Kings 17 where the woman had little meal but made the cake anyway for Elijah? Well, I have learned when giving from the heart, we can never out-give God!

Proverbs 9:10 "The fear of the Lord is the beginning of wisdom: and the knowledge of the holy is understanding."

I Kings 17:15 "And she went and did according to the saying of Elijah: and she, and he, and her house, did eat many days. 16. And the barrel of meal wasted not, neither did the cruse of oil fail, according to the word of the Lord, which he spake by Elijah."

The photos below, of the rose and the female downy woodpecker are small reminders we can't max out our blessings. Look around, there are blessings awaiting…

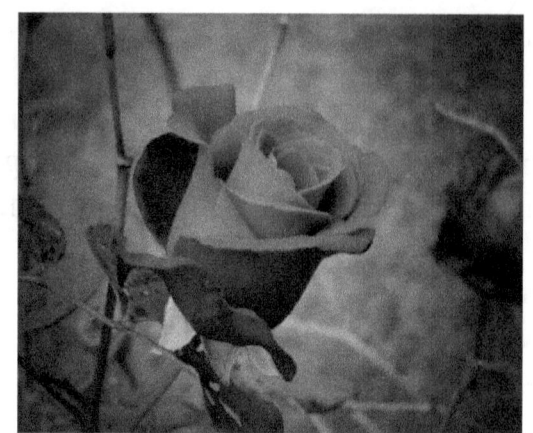

"His Signature"

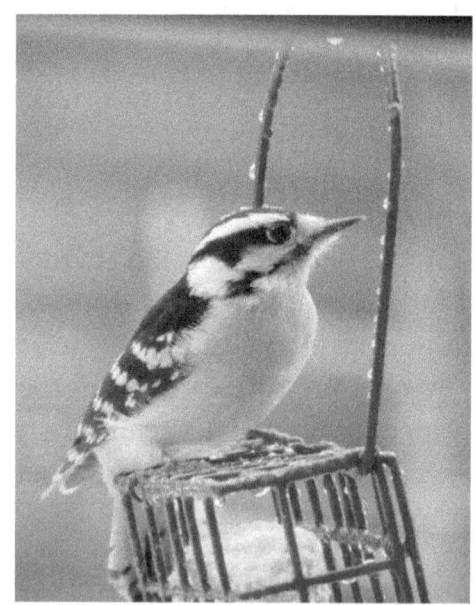

"A Snowy Day Visitor"

~~~

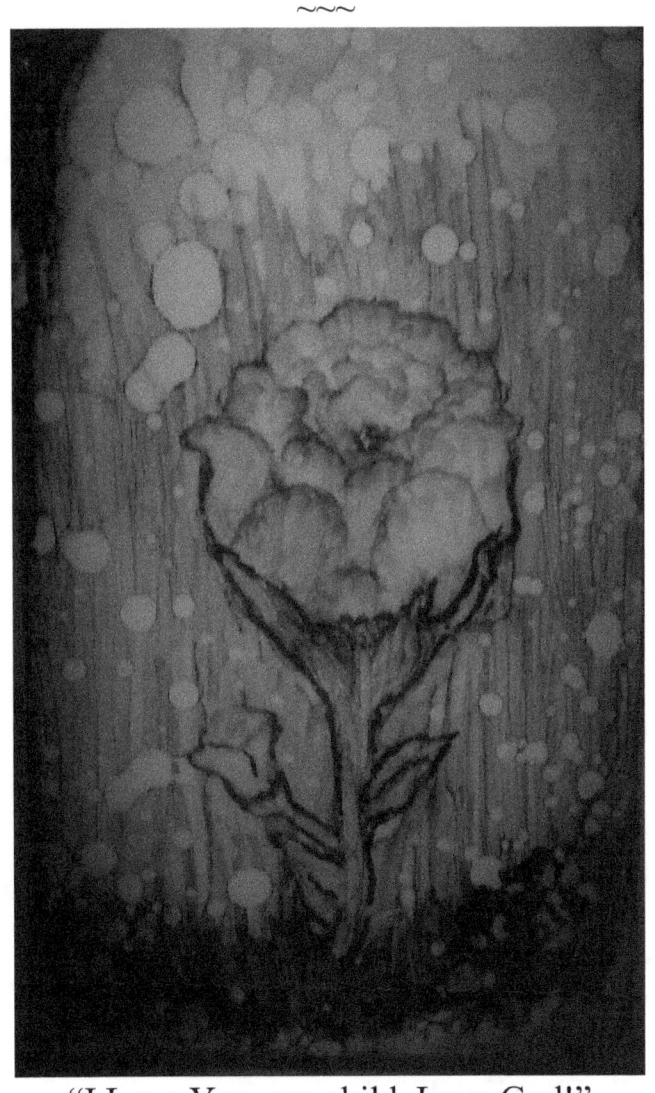

"I Love You, my child, Love God!"
-alcohol ink

~~~

Nanna is Off to the Gym:

I joined the gym, today
OH! What an experience...
I must say!
    At this age, I'm not so tough
but at the look of those scales
enough is enough!
    I have made excuses and excuses
for the way I eat
but in reality...I am in defeat!
    Hey! Look-out fitness center
here comes a grandma with the mindset
I'm Your Next Winner!
    I may be over fifty
and have parts of me
that rub together or sag,
    I am going to win at this...
WAIT... Let me get my bag.
    My bag of courage, that is!
That keeps me going
when life throws me a quiz.
    Some quiz, this is going to be!
I am determined to be healthier
just wait and see
    Christmas is coming,
Christmas is near

Oh, What a feeling...
to be thinner this year!
  I know the director is going to tell me,
It is water I must drink
OH! How my heart will sink!
  Sodas and sweet teas have been "my friend"
I know I have got to make better choices
telling these sugary drinks, this is the end!
  YES, YES, YES to the water,
It's only going to make me flatter
and so much hotter!
  Well, maybe not so much hotter,
younger or smarter just healthier
and a whole lot wealthier.
  Think of the money I have spent
on unhealthy food.
All because...of my mood!
  What do I do with this stash;
I have hidden?
To it, I must bid Goodbye ...Good ridden!

~~~

Nurturing Includes Self

  If I told you I have an addiction to sugar, you
would probably sigh and say to yourself, "Yea,
who doesn't?" If we looked at the statistics of
the number of people addicted to sugar in
correlation to the number of people addicted to a

street drug or opioids, I am curious what the results would be? I read where sugar is like cocaine per (www.brainmdhealth.com/bog/what-do-sugar-and-cocaine-have-in-common/). It is no wonder I feel like an addict with cravings, along with the highs and lows.

If we research the internet, I am sure we could learn quickly the states that are high in addiction rates (www.americanaddictionrates) and the states, high in obesity (https://www.cdc.gov/obesity/data/ prevalence-maps.html) But… Why, are so many people addicted?

Why… Why... WHY? What are we really searching for...peace and/or comfort? Is this a form of denial not wanting to deal with reality? Could this possibly be a veil to hide behind? We hear of sugar substitutes, is unhealthy eating a substitute for prayer time? How often have we used food for a prayer substitute? What are we as a nation doing to improve these high rates? How about per state, per community, per friend or family member? What are we doing to help ourselves? We know we are responsible for our own health/well-being! Yet, for some reason we think it won't happen to us… heart disease, stroke, diabetes, or cancer. (refer to previous internet sites)

For some reason, we continue to harm ourselves! I could make excuse after excuse and I have. The fact is I do not take time to take care of myself! Self-maintenance has not been a priority, although it should have been! Just like those who are addicted, when people told me how bad sugar was for my body, I wasn't willing to give it up until I began having health issues. I Thank God for sparing my life!

I live in a rural area in one of the most beautiful states in America. However, the rocky terrain makes it somewhat difficult daily to exercise outdoors in the winter, unlike living near walking trails, the coastline, etc.

The mother hen, you know the one who carries the nurturing-title, tends to think she must adhere to the care of others even after her children are grown. It doesn't matter if they are her children or not that have a need, we mother hens find it of great importance to feel needed by someone! There is nothing wrong with that thought, long as we do not forget we fall into that category! Our bodies need to be taken care of as well! Like the fitness director said, "When we neglect ourselves, then years down the road when we start to see the signs of poor maintenance we shouldn't be surprised!"

Approximately a month ago I began feeling the symptoms of a heart attack, but like many others, I ignored the signs or blamed them on my gall bladder. I even dismissed the idea and thought maybe they were due to not drinking enough water. I then began to think of all, I mean ALL, of the deserts I have made over the years and enjoyed; and ALL the sodas and sweet teas I have consumed. How foolish I was to think these foods wouldn't one day affect me!

My family's health history has also played a role in my decision to make a positive change in my life. The determination of some of my family members whom have reduced their intake of unhealthy foods and added exercise to their daily regimen have inspired me to make that change! The little sister inside of me screams, "You can NOT let your older brothers win at this challenge! Honestly, I am proud of them for their willpower and perseverance! My daughter has been very inspiring as well, encouraging me to make healthier choices. She and her colleagues conducted a long-term study involving healthier eating. I know I have got to get control! I want to be here for my children and grandchildren and be able to care for my family. We can have a support group with any addiction but until we decide we are ready for that change, sadly their encouragement is ignored!

The morning came that I was scheduled for the interview with the fitness center owner you just read about and I almost cancelled. I was fearful I would not be able to control my addiction/ poor eating habits. I knew I needed the support, the social interaction and the exercises. I also knew my responsibilities at home. When I was late for the interview, I was grateful he was willing to work with me! One of his requirements was for me to press toward my goal, making time to do self-maintenance. I didn't go into a great deal of detail why I was late, I did tell him I have a son with differing abilities that counts on me daily.

That morning consisted of taking our showers at our neighbors due to our bathroom being renovated. We had construction workers that morning, working in a different area of the house. Of course, the phone rang, and I had to wait for someone, (for many times she waited for me when I was a kid). I had to stop for gas, run important errands, and then meet Curt and his worker. We don't always plan for delays and some things we don't remember until the last minute. This reminds me of the time I took Curt to a doctor's appointment. The receptionist had no clue what my morning was like before getting to the window to sign him in. I had written about that day, but that story never made it in these books.

There have been times which you will read about in Volume Two, that I couldn't be counted on due to responsibilities at home, so I erased my name from lists and found myself like an introvert at times then nightly finding myself indulging in unhealthy snacks.

I know this opportunity to go to the gym is a privilege many don't have. I'm thankful for the six hours a day, two days a week I have someone to help-out with my son. It has been two years since he had a worker. I sure hope this schedule will work out with her schedule! It is imperative that I be present at the orientation as well as the trainings. I must take better care of myself so I can take better care of my family!

The pep talk, from a stranger, also awakened me as how slothful I had been. I now have a stronger desire to make healthier food choices, not only for myself but for our family. After getting accepted into the program I began researching the internet how foods with added sugar affect the brain and the body. I remembered once before when I participated in a fifteen-day challenge, how much clearer I could think and how I could reason better after cutting the carbs and sugar back. Seems I could think with more clarity! A Google site sure enough confirmed my remembrance. (https://www.verywellmind.com-how-sugar-affects-the-brain) stated, "excess sugar impairs both our cognitive skills and our self-control, (having a little sugar stimulates our brain for more)". I would highly recommend if you have a problem with this addiction, do your homework and research the facts.

So, like those addicted to drugs, we too can have ups and downs, relapse and fight cravings, go into treatment, relapse, go into treatment, fight cravings...no matter how many times we fail we MUST not stay on the cold ground in defeat! It takes self-determination, support from our friends and family, and strength from God to keep us known as the overcomers, the ones freed from addiction!

I once spoke to a mother whose son was addicted and shared with her how happy I was to hear he was in rehab and how proud she must be of him. She really touched me when she replied, "I used to say I am proud of him but now I say I am proud of my God for how He has given him another chance."

The day after writing this I was reminded about priorities. If we purpose in our heart to be persistent to get to the gym three hours a week, then why can't we purpose in our hearts to get to the Church house at least three hours a week. For there, we should have support, gain strength, most definitely exercise our lungs, and possibly our arms and legs. Spiritual food, couldn't get much healthier food than that! Oh my...

~~~

Here I am Again Lord...

The day of orientation finally arrived! The day, I had anticipated, yet was nervous about being with a crowd of people I did not know. However, I had my new gym shoes ready, anxious to be a part of a program I so desperately needed. As my son and I waited in the car we watched each one entering with the same goal in mind as me. I wondered what they would look like when they met their goals and what their stories were, or if they were even able to share them? As the time grew closer and closer to the start time and the parking lot getting almost full, I began to realize my plans had failed. To be honest, I became upset and frustrated, realizing that once again, I had to erase my name from a list! I knew I had to keep those emotions tucked away and my words intact especially as I looked over and saw a young man full of courage and happiness, my son. Many times, his smile and courage have made me realize I should be more thankful!!! When I first heard of this program, I was under the impression I could go on my time schedule. I didn't know there would be specific days and times until I went for the interview. I was hopeful these hours would work, however, they didn't as you have read. It would not have been fair to Curt to go inside the gym and set while I took the training. And with his needs I couldn't have stayed focused on the goals while there.

I am happy to report the frustrations didn't dampen my desire! I have since began cutting back foods with added sugar and am happy to see the results! I feel so much better and the scales are less in number now! I sleep better, wake up with anticipation for the day ahead. I have much more energy, the brain fog has lifted, the bloating is gone. My memory has improved, even the GERD (heartburn) is gone. My old jeans and I have even renewed our friendship! I can't believe the difference in the way I feel! Label reading and meal planning are vital! This *Christmas gift from God*, I recently referred to is a healthier life He knew I was need of.

Who knows maybe there was a reason for the failed plans that day? We don't always know why things happen the way they do, we do know God gives us vigorous amounts of strength to be overcomers and it is up to us how much of that strength we choose to accept. I am thankful for the information for better health ideas and the healthy recipes I have received from this program. As you will read "Life's Trail" (little later in this book) sometimes we have no clue why paths cross. Here I am again Lord... trusting more fully in You!

I rarely hear of fitness programs specifically for people with differing abilities. Who knows maybe this book will enlighten others to offer programs to people with differing abilities, along with their parents and/or care-takers, so more parents like myself can go to the gym. Maybe this idea of advocacy should be added to my bucket list? (Fitness programs for people with differing abilities)

As you have read, a little sugar intake makes one think he or she needs more. It has been approximately two months since I decided to make healthier choices. Then came the day I was very busy, and I didn't take time to eat a healthy breakfast. I was traveling and found a small candy bar in the car and YES, I ate it! I felt okay afterwards but still hungry. Little did I know, later that night I would have an adult temper tantrum, wanting my way. No, I didn't lay on the floor kicking and screaming but I might as well have. I was having myself a pity party and wanted to pacify myself with comfort food. I not only ate one, but two fresh made cinnamon rolls topped with icing, white chocolate chips and half of a candy bar broken into pieces. (Like a half would have really mattered at that point.) I was so determined to eat that fresh, hot cinnamon roll, I scorched my tongue and dealt with that irritating feeling for several days. No, I didn't stop with the cinnamon rolls. I found some cheesecake in the refrigerator and topped it off with pie filling. I wanted my way! This episode later reminded me of a child like behavior known as a tantrum. I am thankful God renews our minds daily and still loves us even when we have meltdowns. The next day I was back on track...

~~~

Are We Like the Rose?

As I watched the roses begin to unfold today, I thought of how God watches us throughout our lives. The roses outside our windows seemed to have taken longer to bloom this year.

Sometimes patience is all we need for their arrival! I was beginning to think this is not a good year for them, but when I least expected it, yesterday I saw buds, then today their beauty is breath taking. Yesterday, on one bud I saw a June-bug and today on that beautiful blossom I saw the effects of where the bug had been. But the flower never gave up, it bloomed anyway. On another, I saw raindrops from last night's rain but that only enhanced the beauty. I guess what I am trying to say is, no matter what comes against us, we need to be patient. For one day others will see a beautiful rose in us that has been waiting to evolve no matter the challenges we face. One also may be watching as we unfold, identifying our faith in God.

~~~

You Are Living Your Testimony Daily

Several months ago, God whispered, "Don't be troubled over the things you have been through for through those things you have been a testimony for me! How could you or would you be able to tell others how I brought you through if you had not gone through them? How could you be able to reach out if you did not learn how

I was there for you? It is because of your faith and trust in me that you are a survivor!"

Recently I heard a preacher say, "People are watching how we react to whatever the situation is that we are going through". I was thinking this morning of how wonderful it is to know that God knows my heart: the pile of shattered pieces that once was scattered across the floor but are now in-tact, the confined spaces or secret places that once had me imprisoned but now are free, the agonizing cries He heard like a Father who knows His child and now my desire to please Him! Yes, I will be the first to tell you I fail but He truly knows the depth of the love I have for Him. In having love for Him, I want to do all I can to serve Him! When we show others love, this is one way of serving Him. When we serve Him no matter our circumstances, people take notice!

Talebearing, gossiping, backbiting, etc are not ways of loving Him but ways to hurt Him and others. May we be so in love with Jesus that when people hear our name, they immediately think of our testimony of how He brought us through and how we were mindful of others, not how we backbite others.

We all have been guilty at some point of letting our words escape without stopping them.

So, if we have a battle with talebearing or gossiping He will forgive and longs for us to cease this sinful nature! We must pray for strength to overcome and make a conscious effort to do better. Sincerely asking God for forgiveness as well as others leaves quite a lasting impression. Try to avoid being in crowds or with people where this happens, making a conscious choice to speak positive words and refraining from negative comments or even comments that are factual concerning another. There are times especially in the workplace we cannot escape, however we can turn a deaf ear and let our light shine by not joining the conversations. I have found when I spend time alone with Christ, I am more careful with my words. Is this a battle you face? He will equip us if we desire!

Proverbs 26:20 "Where no wood is, there the fire goeth out: so where there is no talebearer, the strife ceaseth."

Proverbs 6:16-19; James 1:22; 2:18,26;

~~~

A Cleaner Environment Leads to a Healthier Life

I am not thinking of "pollution" as we usually refer to it (environmental) but rather as belittling or negative word choices. We need to use positive words, encouraging and uplifting others. Being in an environment where people are genuinely happy is much easier to breath in. Judgmental attitudes, bitterness and low self-esteem can cause pollution in our environments and cause unhealthy relationships.

Recently hearing negative comments from one person to another or from one person about another made me cringe, thinking of how powerful those words are and how deep they cut into one's self esteem. Let us be more mindful of our Christian duties and not partake in these schemes of the devil. Lord, control our thoughts, our words, our actions! How many times have you and I subjected others to an unhealthy environment due to lack of self-control? Self-Control Matters!!!!

While being on the subject, of talking too much, we also need to be mindful that we are not to be self-consumed, esteeming ourselves higher than another. Pride, arrogance, and boastfulness are also a scheme of the devil.

Have you ever met people who crow with pride not just in the morning but throughout their day? Have you ever wished you had a rooster collar to gift them with?

Has there ever been a time you and I have needed a rooster collar? Humbleness Matters....

James 4:17 "Therefore to him that knoweth to do good, and doeth it not, to him it is sin."

II Cor. 4:8,9,17,18, 12:20,21; II Cor. 13:11; James 5:9; I John 4:20; Phil 2:14,15; Galatians 6:7,9; Romans 12.

~~~

Did You Come to Preach?
(a little humor)

Remember in the beginning of the book where you read someone suggested a little more seasoning, a little more about myself? Well, she seemed to think this story for some reason needed to be added. Like I said, I can laugh at myself now.

I believe we should visit other Churches whenever we aren't having service at the church we attend. So, on this night, she, my son Curt and I were off to a church in another county approximately forty-five minutes away. The church was in revival that week and who doesn't love revivals? When we arrived, the parking lot was crowded, and I thought WOW it is going to be a good service tonight! So, I grabbed my Bible and off we went to worship.

My friend was having problems with her knee, so she was walking slowly behind us. Curt on the other hand was raring to go. I could barely keep up with him. Once we got through the parking lot and up the walkway to the door, I looked inside to try to spot an empty area in a pew for us to sit, kind of stalling awaiting my friend to catch up. Boy, was I surprised when my eyes caught a glimpse, of a casket and flowers, near the pulpit! Here I stood with a Bible under my arm, looked as though I was ready to preach at someone's wake that I did not even know. Evidently someone in that community had passed away and the revival was cancelled that night. You should have seen us as we made our way back down that walkway and through the parking lot. Embarrassment was one word I had written all over my face, I am sure. In, reality, that person had already preached his or her own funeral by the life he or she lived. I suppose the moral of this story is, the legacy we leave behind cannot be told in a few hours by someone else. We preach our own funeral by the way we live our daily life... Let's, live it well.

~~~

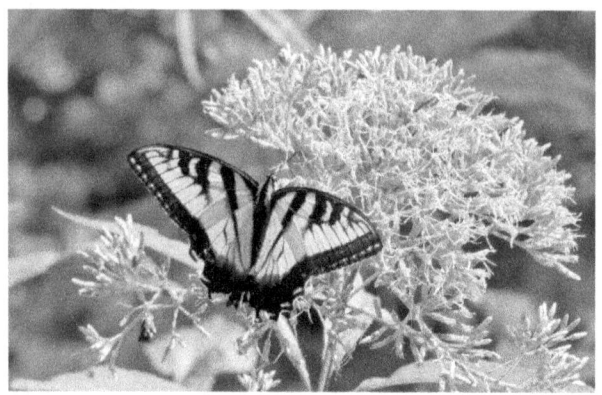
"Crossing Paths with Nature"

Life's Trail

Picture this scene in your mind... walking on a dirt road through the country... with magnificent beauty along the way... which includes works of art from the greatest artist of all times, God. Listen to the sounds of nature… think of the people you have met, for within this place there is contentment.

Although there is beauty, I sometimes feel anxiety that triggers fear. Then I recall so many times before how God walked with me and often carried me when the road was too rocky and steep. Through those times I learned I can trust that He will not lead me astray.

Thinking of how people have come in my life and then they were gone, reminds me of a stranger sojourning or passing by on their way home. It may have felt like a "Hi, how are ya" or they may have stopped and visited for the day or stayed awhile but parting was part of His plan; not really knowing if God purposely sent them to me, or me to them.

I believe we all have a calling on our lives, and we need to be content and appreciate the artwork around us; whether it is nature or people. We do not know why we cross paths with others. There is a reason. There is a plan.

May we never be too busy on this road of life to let others know they are loved. The giving of ourselves outweighs material gifts every time! Can you think of something you saw or someone you met today who touched your life in a unique way?

Ephesians 4:32 "Be kind to one another, tender-hearted, forgiving each other, just as God in Christ also has forgiven you."

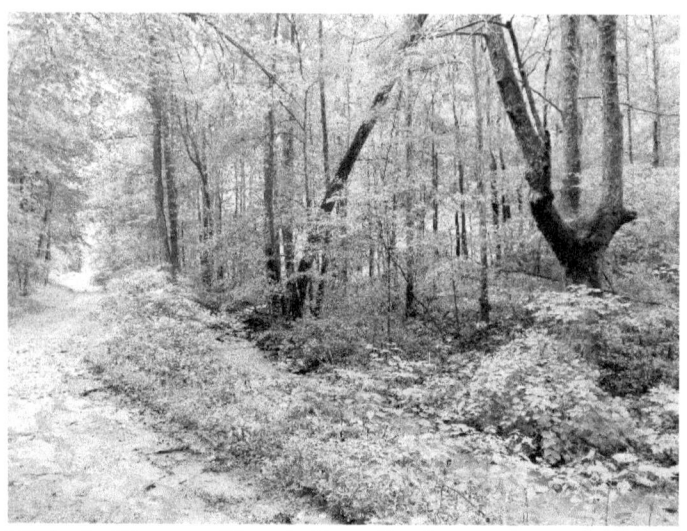

This is Drews Creek Road where my mother and her siblings traveled on foot, to and from school. Mom has told many stories of her family traveling this road.

One story that I was told was when granny who was a mother of fourteen children, walked all the way to the nearest little town. (I am unsure how many miles that was.) She intended to get a few groceries not knowing grandpa had told the store owner to stop all charging for a certain time period. The store owner's family felt so bad for granny they invited her to eat dinner with them before she began her long walk back home.

~~~

A Mother's Prayer

This prayer was inspired from a prayer I carried in my purse for years, unsure who wrote the original prayer. Many years ago, a coworker gave me the prayer on a large index card and suggested I read it and cover my children and grandchildren daily with the prayer.

My Father in Heaven:
I thank You, God for my children, for their health and their uniqueness! Lord, I truly believe they are unique for a reason, and through their uniqueness may others see You. I thank You for trusting me to be their mother and for those who taught me about You, so I would have a basic understanding how to teach my children. Also, for the lessons I have learned through parenting. I believe however You will teach them more effectively and precisely than I ever could. I am trusting You with their lives and souls, believing one day we will all be together forever.

I pray God that they would keep that hunger for Your word embedded in their hearts. You said, Your Word would not return to You void and to train them up and they will not depart. May they always be able to discern Your voice, recognizing the importance of studying Your word, helping them to become rooted and grounded producing visible fruits of the spirit. Through learning the sound of Your voice, may they come to know You are there amidst, their trials, finding comfort and peace.

Lord, I pray they would desire Your gifts as they strive to become a pillar in the Church where You have led them. A place where they can worship and praise You freely and encourage others along the way. I pray You give them understanding of when and how to speak Godly knowledge, the discernment of when evil is present, the faith that keeps them knowing You, are, their ever-present help; as well as other gifts to help them stay humble, edifying the church which is the body of Christ.

May they recognize and abstain from stumbling blocks that were self-placed such as: pride, lust, ignorance due to not studying, or idols. I ask You, please Lord, to give them a zeal and desire to make conscious decisions based on Your word. Please God remind them when temptations come of who sent those temptations and what repercussions they will endure if they are not submissive to Your word. May they be examples to their children and other children not displaying slothfulness, but Godliness in all forms.

God, I ask if at any time they be discouraged that You would place Christians in their paths or angels to uplift them and remind them that they are chosen and loved. I think of the scripture in Psalms 139, how You knew them well before I did and how You fashioned them and of Your loving thoughts toward them. I pray God for their protection as they go about their daily lives and others would grace them with favor. These are our babies (Yours and mine) Lord, Thank You for loving them and sparing them time!!!! Thank You for allowing me to birth them and watch them grow!

I praise You for all that You have done and the favor You have shown them. May they show favor to others, blessing people whole heartedly, not grudgingly. May they use the battles we have faced as a family or in their adult lives as learning tools to show compassion to others.

Lord, I pray if they do not know You personally may they come to know that peace that only You can give, and may they seek your grace/forgiveness wholeheartedly and appreciate every aspect of You. I truly believe I need to cover them daily with prayer. In Jesus name, Amen.

While praying, I not only call out my children's names but my family's names as well.

Hebrews 4:16 "Let us come boldly unto the throne of grace, that we may obtain mercy, and find grace to help in time of need."

II Timothy 2:22 "Flee also youthful lusts: but follow righteousness, faith, charity, peace, with them that call on the Lord out of a pure heart."

Romans 6:7 "For the wages of sin is death; but the gift of God is eternal life through Jesus Christ our Lord."
I Cor. 2:5; John 3:17; II Peter 3:9-18; I John 1:19;
II Cor. Chap. 12 and 14

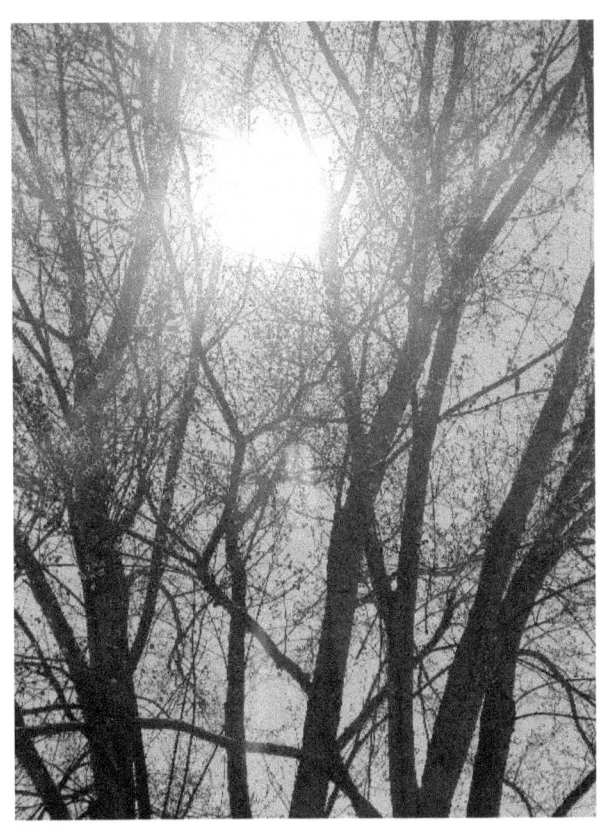

"Pray for America!"
When I snapped this photo, I never imagined
there would be a cross with the sun in the
middle. In color, this is red (sunrays), white (the
sun) and blue (the sky). Reminded me of how
we need to pray for our nation!!!

~~~

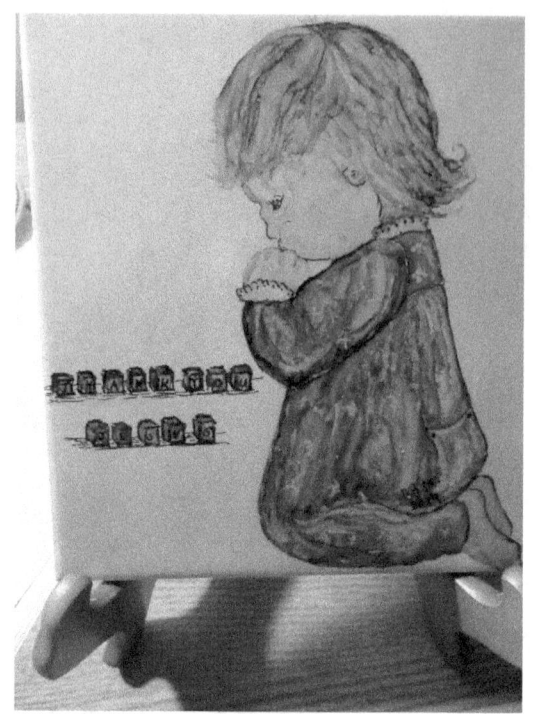

"Let's be more childlike...forgiving and
humble." -alcohol ink

~~~

Do We Smell Like the Sheep?

I heard a sermon about how a shepherd cares
for his flock. The minister spoke of the
shepherd and how the shepherd should smell
like the sheep for if he is a good shepherd
tending his flock, he will smell like them for he
cared enough to be near them. Aren't you
thankful for those shepherds whom smell like

us? We all know a shepherd has a full plate from caring for his family, to caring for his flock as well as listening to many opinions and hearts' cries, studying, visiting. Some work full time jobs while working the spiritual fields. Yet, when a shepherd fails, what do we do? Have we placed them on a pedestal expecting great things? They are human, too! Then I thought, how well do we, as siblings in Christ care for our fellow sheep? Could that be where the word, "fellowship" originated from?

Romans 14:12 "So then every one of us shall give account of himself to God."

~~~

Loneliness is Natural

As you have read, I am a single mom and have been for ten years. I find writing our feelings helps us to face them. I want to thank God for where I am today, and it is only because of Him that I can feel this peace and joy. I am human and do experience lonely times and it is during those times that I feel that bond becoming stronger between the Lord and me.

Loneliness to me is an emptiness or a void, even though one is in a room full of people one can still feel alone! Being married to my best friend for over twenty years, then came the painful separation/divorce process, then all the sudden one day he was gone, what an empty feeling that was! I went to the places we loved to go, the beach, the mountains and on a train ride and could imagine his presence but his hand was not there to hold nor his smile there to melt my heart. Not being able to say goodbye or to allow my feelings to come out in those three little words that mean so much is a deep regret. I was hurt and bitter because of the choices he was making and never realized I still loved him until the day I heard he was pronounced dead. Emptiness... loneliness.... abandonment... so many emotions and feelings! The shattered pieces are now healed. Dreams still come and memories now bring more laughter than tears.

Now as I watch our children taking on the role of adulthood and our grandchildren playing and giggling, I thank God for allowing me to be at this point in my life. Oh, by the way, one of the best gifts a child could give his or her parents are grandchildren, Thank You, Josh!

I do still miss Saul (my late husband). Perhaps a part of me will always grieve for what I wish could have been. I have chosen to be thankful for the time we did have and am improving in letting go of the questions. I am ready now to move on with my life. When our family is together, we still laugh and we still rejoice, within and among the joyous sounds of love, especially at Christmas, he is there in our midst.

I went through the motions but was empty inside, wondering how I would make it through these new demands, new responsibilities, new kind of aloneness. How would I be able to console our children and answer their questions? The separation was painful, similar, to a death. Then his actual death was like trauma to the most inner part of my heart!

I do thank God for comfort and for hearing my heart's cry day after day. Saul's memory does not reside in a painful place any longer, but rather lives in a place of peace and sweet remembrance in my heart. His desire to make others laugh still makes my heart smile.

I have learned we have to let go of the past. We must toss aside the baggage (hurt, sadness, bad memories...) that can weigh us down. Yet it is okay to treasure the good times that were had. Although writing those words are easier than letting go! However, let go of the PAST! Don't dwell there. Start looking for the simple things that bring us joy each day. Let's load our wagons with kind deeds, new beginnings and joy. How about doing kind deeds for those who can't repay us?

Loneliness is natural but we do not have to live there! Satan will keep that "L" word replaying in our head if we will allow him to along with other negative thoughts. I know that for a fact! Happiness is our choice! God said, He would renew our minds daily, let's remind Satan of that! I am ashamed to say it took me years to realize the culprit behind all the negative thoughts. Once I realized and called him out, I found happiness, inner peace and contentment.

These simple things helped me press on for the joyful journey ahead and keep my mind's focus where it needed to be, in the future and not wander back to the pain of the past:
*Being in the presence of the Lord...
*My children's laughter, our time together: If only you all knew the depth of my love for you!
*Time with my grandchildren, unless you are a grandparent you will never understand that kind of love. It is like getting a second chance to be a parent. Oh, to be a part of their creative play, imagination, innocence and quirky word usage.
*Time with my family especially when they are fun spirited.
*Conversations with the elderly...

*When I have time to explore my talents...
*Going to serene places, the mountains, the riverbank, farms....
*When I hear from old friends that I have not seen or heard from in a while, I guess that is an attribute of social media. However, I would much rather hear from them in person or their voice via telephone.

Hebrews 12:1 "Wherefore seeing we also are compassed about with so great a cloud of witness, let us lay aside every weight, and the sin which doth so easily beset us, and let us run with patience the race that is set before us."

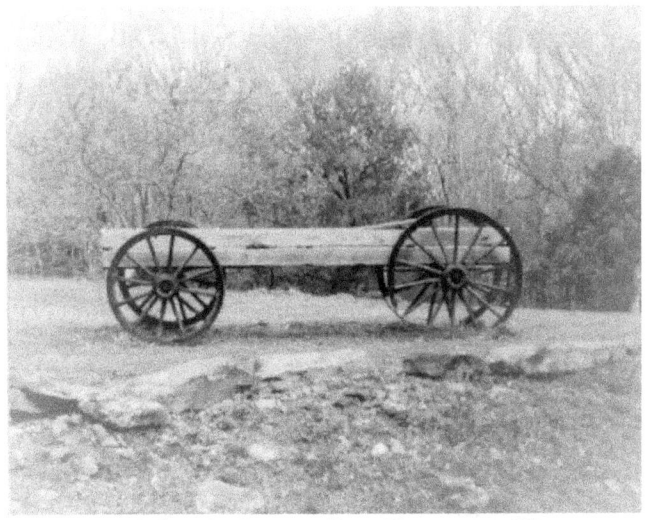

"What's in…. "yer" wagon?"

~~~

The Life of a Gardener

When I was in the garden today, I thought of how we need to remove the rocks in our lives that keep the roots of the good crops from growing deeper, allowing us to have a closer, stronger relationship with God. The rocks can be things which are hard to let go of like addictions, idols, hurt, and/or guilt. The weeds need removed as well, which not only steal nourishment from the crops but also allow snakes to hide in. The weeds we allow to grow can be things such as: jealousy, bitterness, and/or hatred. The snakes can be things such as: temptations, depression.

Sometimes we plant and/or waters the seed and someone else sees the harvest. The crops we plant can be such things as kindness, compassion, and love. We are all caretakers of our own gardens (lives), may we be more attentive to the weeds and rocks so our gardens will be beautiful and admired. What kind of a harvest are you expecting?

As I go daily to the vegetable garden to look for growth and weed out the unwanted, I think of the growth I see in my Christian siblings. I do not think we should compare our gardens, though. We all mature differently, depending on our farming skills.

Just recently our neighbors' garden was plowed, and the seeds and plants were planted and not hardly any weeds did I see. The ones I saw, the gardener was working diligently to remove them. They had spread straw to reduce the growth of weeds.

Think of how we could improve our spiritual garden? What if others were observing our garden? Do we wear garden gloves and garden shoes, or do we carelessly go about our work? Garden shoes? We all need a pair of them! "Why?" You may ask? For when we put on our garden shoes, we are purposely setting out to do a work. Often, the work we are called to do might involve laboring and toiling through rough grounds.

What kind of seeds did we plant today? Oh, what about our seeds? Do we gather from the Bible daily, or do we use old seeds from years past? Are we planting daily or are we leaving the seeds set for a more convenient time to sow? In Mark 4:2-9 Jesus taught by parables of how sowing seeds can reap a harvest. But seed sown on stony ground has no depth so it withers and dies; and seed sown among the thorns is choked by them and seed that fall by the wayside the seeds will be eaten by the fowls. Verse 8: "And other fell on good ground, and did yield fruit that sprang up and increased; and brought forth, some thirty, some sixty, and some an hundred." Think of how it took a dark period to make the seed grow...the dark times in our lives change us as well. What we consider a dry spell God considers a growing season!

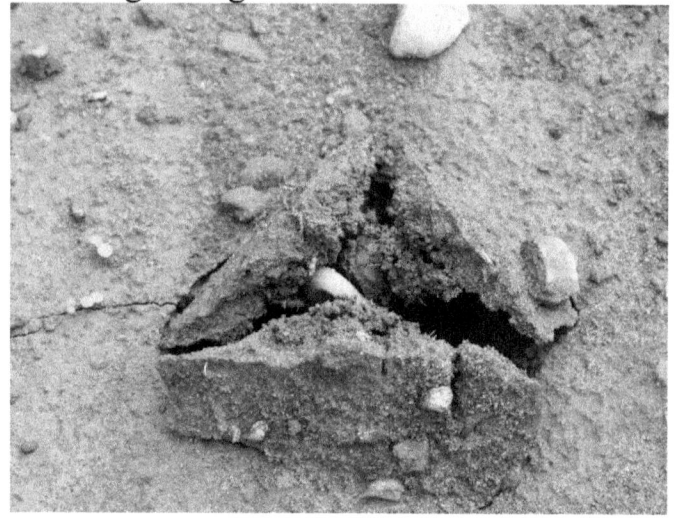

"The Stages of Growth"

John 4:34-38

~~~

A Letter to My Sisters in Christ, Whom, are Single

Dear Sisters,

Be Authentic! Be happy where you are!
Whether you are a stay at home mom or a
presenter traveling the country! When you have
learned to love yourself and become strong in
the Lord, for it is only through Him you live and
move and can do all things. Then you may be
ready to allow that God fearing man to unlock
your heart.

Someone once told me to make a wish list
for the kind of man I would like to have in my
life. Well, a couple of years ago I did just that
and the list keeps getting longer! I am trusting
the Lord, for His timing is always best. You may
find this humorous, but I am really thinking of
adding a specific sports store shopper to my
wish list. I was parked in the parking area of
this store and could not help but notice the
number of men who opened doors for their
wives or girlfriends. I was really impressed! I
cannot say they were one hundred percent
genuine in his gentlemanly behavior or was just
eager to get to do some shopping in said store!!!
They sure were impressive though. Think I may
add one... *A gentleman who opens my door*!

Some say they become cynical after years of
being single. I would consider the word,
"wiser", a better descriptive word. As we age
and learn from insincere relationships, we gain

knowledge and wisdom, becoming more cautious with who we allow within the walls we have carefully built around our hearts. Dating at this age one must be more prayerful, mindful, observant, cautious and extremely patient.

We most certainly need to take time to heal before entering a new relationship! Carrying baggage from a previous relationship that we can't seem to let go of only makes the new relationship cumbersome, awkward or difficult. Jealousy, anger, guilt, bitterness, rejection, and trust issues are baggage we need to deal with, pray over and leave behind.

Remember some men are looking for a pretty face and not commitment. If we stay committed to God, we will be Beautiful to the right man, in God's time, if it is His will for us to have a mate. If you meet a charming, handsome, hard-working, good ole fellow, I suggest you pray for direction. I mean PRAY! He will not want you to sacrifice your Christian values! Do NOT fall into Satan's snares! Keep your Christian values in the forefront, if he is meant for you, he will respect you! Better yet, he will lead and guide you to the Lord, together you two will make a beautiful team!!! Otherwise, consider him a friend and continue your search....

A seasoned, single woman, who has been single quite a few years is similar to a banker. If we both see the real American "Bill" long enough, we can spot a counterfeit afar off!

Here is a mental note we need to keep in mind:
Men, if you are not ready to set your priorities straight and put God first ...to be faithful ...to be loyal/committed ...to be honest ...to be devoted ...to have respect ...then Do NOT DISTURB me ...I am waiting on the one who is!

I used to jokingly tell people, when I find the man who is not perfect but perfect for me, I am going to check the bottom of his feet to see if he was dropped from heaven, for he will be my angel! I am still waiting but while waiting I am not sitting around twiddling my thumbs. I want to be about the Lord's work. Romans 8:16 speaks of how our spirit will bear witness with one another. May we not forget the scripture telling us to not be unequally yoked- (II Cor. 6:14).

God also may be preparing us to be that Godly woman our mate is waiting upon. Ladies take care of yourselves and take time to enjoy life! Pray for direction, guidance and listen to His voice with careful attention. Some males are only meant to be friends with you, know the difference. Please respect yourselves and others for you are a Godly woman, a powerful witness, a treasure in God's eyes. Luke 9:5 "And whosoever, will not receive you, when ye go out of that city, shake off the very dust from your feet for a testimony against them." You are chosen, by the Most High, dust yourself off and walk with confidence Sister!

Loneliness can cause one to go to extremes like over-dating. For example, I have seen people who are longing for a male figure in their lives possibly due to not having a father figure growing up. She may compromise her walk with Christ; just knowing this guy is the one, only later to find out, he most definitely was not! These ladies not only ended up hurt but their children were caught up in the web as well. I have also seen women in a financial crisis and marry without waiting to see if they were compatible. I can understand the temptation! That's why we need to encourage our sisters who are single and reach out to them and pray for one another. Recognize the clues when a sister is crying out. It's our responsibility to uplift her, not throw stones!

If you have children, be the kind of mother they honor and respect, teaching them to honor God with their bodies, mind, and spirit.

Integrity MATTERS!!! (1 Cor. 7:34 "The unmarried woman careth for the things of the Lord, that she may be holy both in body and in spirit: ..."). The example we are setting requires modeling not just words alone. I believe less dates with the right men are far better than many dates with the wrong men. Also, we need to be careful about introducing our children to our dates too soon. Allow time to tell, sparing them unnecessary heartaches.

We all know dating in our 40's and 50's is much different than when we were in our teens! There are so much more responsibilities, life experiences causing trust issues, social media to deal with, our roles as parents and caregiver, the middle age spread (sarcastically written). Dating at this age has a whole new meaning. I do not know about you, but I find it difficult to date at this age. Maybe I am old school, I believe in faithfulness and respect. I am learning friendships are what most men are wanting. I have learned, as a mother of an adult child with differing abilities, how this can affect relationships. However, the right man will acknowledge and love all, of my children, understanding they are a part of me. Some men I suppose, are fearful of the unknown. I feel sometimes I have built a wall to prevent anymore hurt to my children. Whatever the reasons we remain single we know we can trust the Lord's timing for His faithfulness has been proven time and again. There is no one who can love us like He can!

Remember the scripture in Psalms 30:5 "...Weeping may endure for a night but joy, cometh in the morning"; hold on, find a hobby, help one another, most of all STAY FOCUSED...we got to help each other make it home!

We all want to be a Proverbs 31 woman or a Titus 2 woman! It takes daily renewing of our minds and dedication!

Matthew 6:26 "Behold the fowls of the air: for they sow not, neither do they reap, nor gather into barns; yet your heavenly father feedeth them. Are ye not much better than they?"

1 Corinthians 6:20 "For ye are bought with a price; therefore, glorify God in your body, and in your spirit, which are God's."

I Timothy 4:12,13 "Let no man despise thy youth, but be thou an example of the believers, in word, in conversation, in charity, in spirit, in faith, in purity."

Romans 14:16 "Let not then your good be evil spoken of:"

Col. 3:22-23; 1 Tim. 6:10-15; II Tim. 2:15-16; I Cor. 7:2-5,8,9; Daniel 3:25; I Cor. 6:14-19; Col. 3:2; Eccles 4:6; Proverbs 3:5-7; Hebrews 11:25; Hebrews 13:6; Mark 14:38; I Timothy 5:8-11,14; James 5:7-11

alcohol ink

~~~

Let Go of the Unicorn

People can say, "Let go of the past", I have said it myself a time or two, truthfully, many times! Sometimes, it takes years to actually let go, though, even if they are tangible objects. I had these books written and ready for editing and have gotten better in the way of grieving, then there it was... "The UNICORN!" I then realized I had held onto that dingy torn stuffed animal for years. Why? I really don't know! Maybe that was a part of Saul I still had. A piece I could cling to although I kept in stored away, I still held on to it mentally.

You see many, many years ago when we were dating, he bought me this big beautiful white unicorn as a gift. I loved it and kept it in my room. That was until he and I would get into an argument! Then I would assure him I no longer wanted that stuffed thing that reminded me of him. Honestly, I must have carried that back to him on several occasions. Because once we were at my parent's back gate and as the unicorn was going across the gate, on his way back around the hill again, we were surprised to see my mom come outside and rescue the unicorn. The unicorn stayed at my home until he and I got married, then went home with us to our little rental home.

Several years after Saul's death, which made the unicorn almost thirty years old, I found the dingy, torn unicorn in our basement. I finally felt like I was ready to let go, but really, I don't think I was. Then, about the time I had taken it to the pile of junk to be taken to the landfill, my sister came around the house and rescued him again. She knew the trail he had been on and wanted to keep that old unicorn in her storage unit until she got her own place. Well, several years passed and once again he returned, back home. Approximately about a month ago (which was about eight and half years since Saul's death), I knew it was finally time to let go of that unicorn for good. In all honesty it was a difficult decision, but I knew the only way to move on is to let go of the past! I knew this time I couldn't go get it back out of that garbage bin even though I had thought about it. Some of us carry baggage for years. The only way to heal is to let go...in our own time that is. For some people that takes years! I think I am finally ready for a relationship. I have asked myself this question for years, "Am I really ready?"

~~~

The Reflection

I am in the process of reading a book about a couple who had been in a horrible crash and for months the lady had not looked in the mirror, fearing the distorted reflection she would find. I wondered how many of us do not like who we see in the mirror or maybe how many of us see beyond that reflection of how broken we were but now see someone different. When we look now, do we see reassurance and triumph? Do we find strong independent women or men longing for others to see beyond the blemishes, scars, etc? I have found to even begin to love again, that one must love herself or himself and the person she or he is now, before others will love her or him. When we feel good about ourselves, not boastfully or being vain, but finding happiness and the kind of joy that only God can give. Then and only then our smiles will be genuine, our compassion will be real, and the love we have will awaken others to see beauty in us. With God in our lives, people will see a difference!

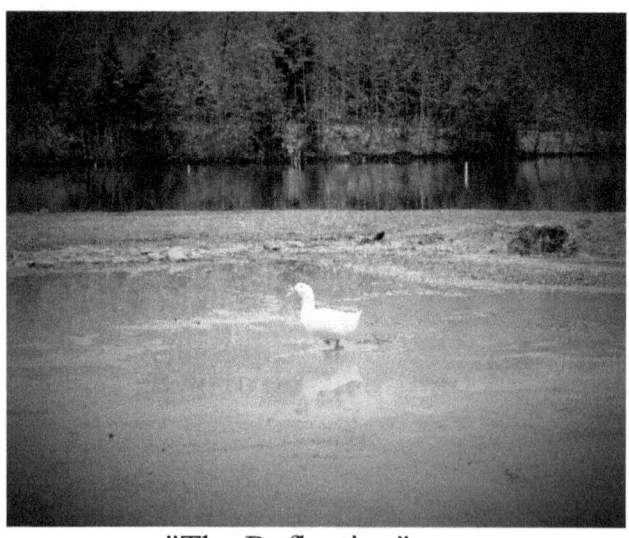

"The Reflection"

~~~

Chocolate, Pride and Durable Tape
(A little more humor)

Let's see, where do I begin... you just read about the reflection in the mirror and we are not to be prideful or vain. You have read about self-discipline and how I battle weight gain due to my love for chocolate. You are about to read how a durable tape, I thought, would come to my rescue.

One day Curt and I were shopping, and I knew we had a social event coming up with our Church family, so I wanted to purchase a new pair of dark panty hose to go along with the dress I was so happy to now fit into. I had worked so hard to get the weight off and was anxious to wear that smaller dress. I soon learned the panty hose aisle was a boring place for my son. He did not want to stand in that section any longer while I looked through all the pairs for the exact kind I was looking for in my new size. Therefore, I finally had to compromise and grab a pair of thigh highs. I knew they would be high enough and the color would work so off we went to finish our shopping.

The day had finally come for the social event and I was excited to get started. I made the food

119

we were planning to take. Then got Curt and I ready, and we were on our way. We finally got to the place and as I was carrying in the food, I felt my thigh highs begin to slide down my white legs. I was frantic, trying to keep them up while trying to be inconspicuous. You can imagine the sight! I did manage to get the food inside and be friendly with everyone before heading back out to find a store that sold real panty hose, no matter what color. I knew there was a store a few miles down the road and there was not much time before the event was to start.

We made it to the store, which we had never been in. I immediately asked the clerk where their panty hose were located, only to find out they did not sell panty hose. I was shocked! I thought they sold about everything in that kind of store! The thought then hit me and I said, can you tell me where a specific kind of tape is? I was hoping she wasn't wondering, or be brave enough, to question what I was up to!

By now we are on our way back up the road only to the sight of me trying to adhere small strips if this shiny, durable tape from my thigh highs to my thighs, while driving. What was I thinking! When I looked over at Curt, I was sure he was wondering what in the world I was doing then he started signing that he wanted some of that tape on his arms. I tried to explain to him, you know the phrase, don't do as I do but do as I say. I must admit this was one time I was glad he couldn't "spill the beans" on me when we got back to the Church function. For you see there was this handsome fellow there I had my eyes on. I wanted to impress him by wearing the dress I hadn't been able to get into and look elegant even with my hidden attachment!

This is where it really gets funny. During the singing people were standing up joining in with the music and worshipping. I love to do that as well, but this time was quite different! The tape that is well known for its durability was coming loose and sticking to my dress, making my dress roll in the areas which was between my knees and my hips. I tried to watch the bathroom door to make sure no one was in there so when I got up, I could make a direct line to get inside and reattach the tape. Needless, to say, I didn't stand up after that and enjoy worshipping because this well known brand of tape, thigh highs and skin don't mingle too well.

Once the event was over, I wanted to make a beeline to the car but being social was a must, so as I was easing out the door, urging Curt along, I smiled and said my goodbyes. That day, I was reminded pride comes before a fall! My worship time now is NOT limited by pride or any other unnecessary attachment! Have you ever allowed pride to hinder your worship?

My oldest son is a firm believer in this kind of tape, and I couldn't wait to tell him I found one thing the tape didn't stick to but was too embarrassed to tell him for I knew he would hound me for days to come. Now, we laugh about my silliness! What are some of your witty moments? We all have them! You know the ones that cause tears to run down your face or your friend's face.

Another brainless moment I had was when I brought a cat home. A cat that has been killed on the road! A cat that looked much like "Rotten" our cat, which had been missing. What a name, huh? I lost my watch that day but didn't realize it until later. When I tell this story, I conclude: the moral of this story is to do a good deed even if we lose track of time. Maybe not by bringing home road kill to be buried. My watch was lying beside the road near where I retrieved someone's cat that later got buried in our backyard.

~~~

A Widow's Letter to Santa

Dear Santa ("Sanna")

This is Nanna, a little too old for a Christmas
wish, maybe so?
Only you would know!

The children are possibly nestled in their
beds, with the thoughts of adulthood running
through their heads.

Meanwhile, I am here writing you this note,
envisioning a Christmas, preparing to lug tote
after tote.

I've been a good ol' girl, cleaning, cooking
and sewing, carrying in the wood;
believing in keeping the upcoming family
traditions alive like all families should.

You see, this year Santa I'd like a change,
I'd like to add a new member
a new "dad" on the range.

My children deserve a Godly man,
who will be there daily, to show compassion and
too understand.

My grandchildren need a jolly ol' soul,
to rumble, laugh and play. My wish is for the
right man to fill the role.

It has been many years, with anticipation I
have waited and waited; and once again our
house will be festively decorated!

May this be the year, I have a baking partner,
a best friend… someone to share my passions
and my life with… until the end.

Oh, won't you save room in your sleigh,
as you pass over the mountains and farms, keep
an eye out if you may.
    You know the one that is rugged, tall and
sweet as can be,
trustworthy, faithful, loyal, a lil' romantic, and a
hard worker is he;
strong, yet gentle and kind,
keeping God first and Heaven on his mind.
    Thank you, Santa for all that you do!
Actually, this is my prayer, and Lord, this should
have been addressed to You!
    As the years have passed,
I have learned patience, trust and an
unconditional love that last.
    I know if it is Your will,
my Christmas wish will soon be here
filling my waiting heart with a cheer.
Love, Nanna

    A man once told me he could love me like
Jesus. Boy, was he quickly corrected! He had
no clue what Jesus had carried me through and
how he had loved me in the darkest times of my
life. A friend and I were talking of how there
are no love like Jesus' love, and we agreed it
would be wonderful to find a fellow who would
try to love us like Jesus does. I think it is natural
to search for a mate. However, in our search we

124

must pray and wait. No, I did not get my Christmas wish and that is okay. My trust of His timing is still the same.

I am now beginning to like single life! I can stay up as late as I want, sew when I want, eat when I want, go whenever I want and speak to whoever I want...no hurry Lord, send the right man whenever you want.

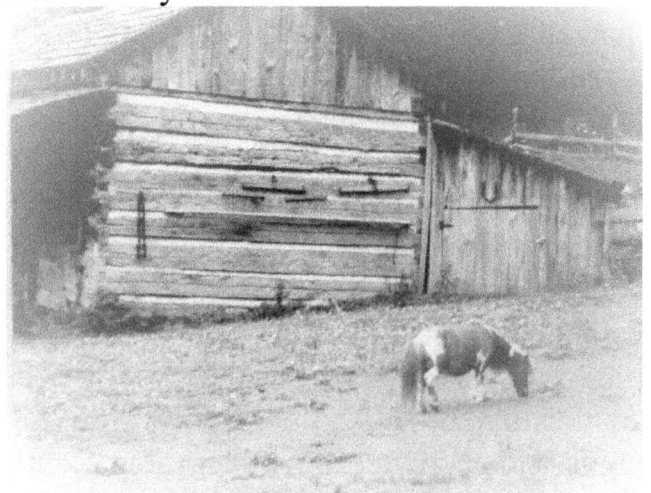

"Sometimes We Must Graze Alone"
It has taken me years to graze alone inside a restaurant. I can now, but for years I wouldn't.

~~~

A Marriage License is NOT an Owner's Permit

I am writing this because hindsight is 20/20 and because I see the woman, I used to be in some of the partners in marriages today. I have also faced some of these issues on my own marriage. I raised my kids in church from the time they were little but being sold out to God was not who I was. I tried to be faithful in church attendance and lived a clean life but was lacking the daily devotion that was needed. I worked a lot, cared for my family, loved my husband and was devoted to him, but can now see myself in some people and want so much to shake them and say STOP! A marriage license is not an owner's permit. Allow your partner to be happy in life!

When one is dominating, manipulating or controlling the other or is prideful, wedges get forced between a relationship. To make a marriage work God must be in the center, good communication, time together, respect and willingness to cooperate are all very important! No matter the circumstance, ridiculing or belittling the other, especially in a crowd or on social media, is a definite no-no. These are tools of the devil!

If a partner is lacking self-esteem, exhausted, jealous or feels unappreciated, he or she may lash out without being able to explain why. Love and take care of each other! Do things for each other to keep the marriage alive, simple things, be creative! Write love notes and leave them. Carry his coffee to him. Wash the dishes for her. Be fair with the to do list and share the jobs. If he works all day have him a hot dinner ready. If she works all day, run her a hot bath. Make decisions together, take walks, hold hands. Cherish your time together! DO NOT allow Satan to destroy your marriage! Trust is essential! Remember the man is the head of the household just as Jesus is head of the Church.

Encourage your mate to take time for things he or she loves, such as hobbies, time with friends or family. Find harmony within! A good balanced life is not giving of yourself all the time. Take time for adventure, hobbies and laughter. Take time to live! You both only have one lifetime. Live it so though there will be no regrets. Don't cling, nor ignore, LOVE with the deepest part of your heart, allowing each other space to soar and renew his or her mind.

Everyone has flaws, pray for your mate! The grass is NOT greener on the other side. If you have hurt him or her or are hurt, communicate/apologize, do not let the hurt fester. Remember spiritual war-fares are of the devil. Cherish, I say "CHERISH" your marriage! Go on dates, keep your marriage alive!

I have friends who are single and due to the unhealthy relationship or marriage they were previously in, they are shell-shocked, fearful of a similar relationship. Contentment and peace of mind outweighs another unhealthy relationship. I have to admit it does get lonely being single for years, take care of that marriage!

Jealousy is like a two-sided mirror. One thinks it is hidden away, an unwanted attachment but others see right through the glass. Jealousy can make one's life miserable and the other person fearful to live a happy normal life. Although once you give that hidden, unwanted attachment that weighs you down to God, life will be so much brighter and easier. I remember when I gave that attachment to God how much better I felt!

By all means... if your spouse has an addiction do all you can to get him or her help! Addiction takes precedence over people or things that was once a priority in their lives. Words and actions can cut you to the core. Help them anyway and every way you can without becoming an enabler. Research, ask questions, find a reliable rehabilitation center that is accountable and credible!

The days of visiting at the rehab centers thinking I was doing a good thing taking our kids there to visit now makes me cringe. I wish they had not seen their dad in his condition, due to the effects of the medication they had him on. After he came home, we successfully detoxed him off the added medications. I would suggest a person seek a doctor's approval before detox. PLEASE, I can't tell you loud enough to research, research, research possible treatment centers! Do all you can to save your spouse's life. Wish I had done more!

It is okay for each of you to have friends, male and female, but be considerate of how your conversations are held, have respect! Remember, you are married, and if you have children, your need for attention or lack there-of, from your spouse causing you to look for another, is detrimental to your children. They may be young however they sense and learn quickly. PLEASE do not hurt them too! I have seen this happen!!!

Love one another but do not idolize your spouse. When you love God first, each other second then your children, your home will be a place of harmony. One day your children will be grown and the bond you and your spouse have created will only get stronger if you follow this chain of command. Decrease your time with technology and increase your time with family. Quality time is the foundation for memories. Marriage takes effort, APPLY THE EFFORT!!

I Corinthians 7:3-5, Titus 2:1-5; Hebrews 13:4; I Peter 3:7-12, Ephesians 5:21-23; 1 Timothy 3:5; II Timothy 2:22;

~~~

Writing My Daily Lesson Plan

When I was a preschool teacher, I had to write daily lesson plans. If I was a teacher now, and my daily life was the lesson, what would I be teaching? Am I the example I need to be? Do I call sin what it is, or do I partake in it? Is my commitment to Christ seen and not just heard?

Lord, help me today to not follow man or woman but follow You and be the example You would be pleased with. Help me stand with authority and power to fight against the snares of the devil. Help me to identify my shortcomings and downfalls and teach others to love.

Luke 10:19; Acts 29:19

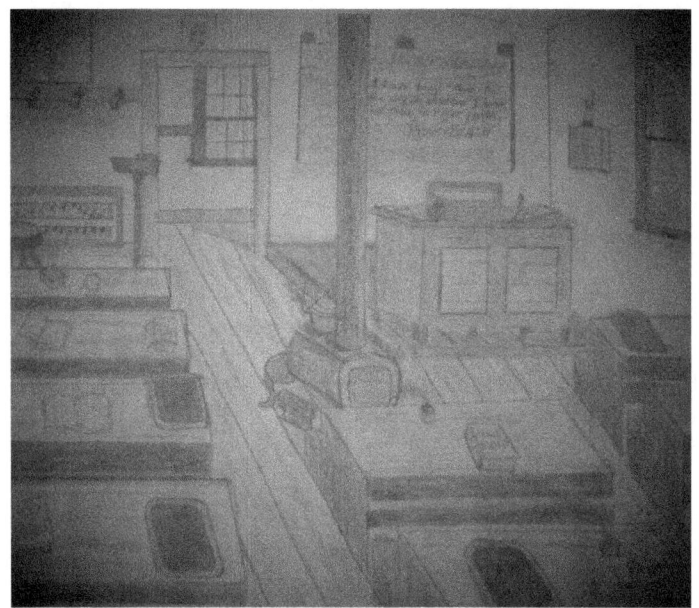

"What Are We Teaching the Children?"

I always found art to be interesting and have been blessed to use that talent to earn extra money when there was more month than money. Original artist unknown, this scene was so appealing to me I sketched it adding Bibles on the desks and a scripture on the board. We desperately need God back in our schools!

Proverbs 4:11 "I have taught thee in the way of wisdom; I have led thee in right paths." This is the scripture written on the chalkboard.

~~~

Weep, Pray, Praise

I write this from one mother to another, as we become burdened for our children or the situations they may be in or the issues they are facing, we can find comfort in God's word. Just recently I was crying out to the Lord and the Holy Spirit was so strong in my car and then later in the kitchen of our home, invisible yet there. I felt as though he was surrounding me like a cloud, a familiar feeling, a feeling of security.

We are to keep the clutter cleared from our minds for the devil likes to hang out there as if it is a playground. If we allow the busy days, they will build blinders and if we neglect time alone with Christ our faith decreases. Therefore, when a trial or a burden comes, we cry out in despair. But if we have an intimate relationship, which requires daily devotion, we are stronger in the Lord, allowing for praise to happen; knowing we can trust Him with our babies and find rest amidst the storm.

Yes, we weep because we love our babies and we pray because we believe from the deepest part of our hearts He will answer. We praise because of the fact He heard us and took us to that resting place. A place of solitude that only can be found in Him. In Matthew 15:28 He spoke to a mother, noting her faith and in

Matthew 12:25 we read how Jesus knew their hearts. We know He has no respect of person! He knows your heart and mine, aren't you glad?

"There's a breaking in my favor...as I pray" were the words in a song I heard just after praying, what perfect timing! I was talking to a friend on the phone, you know the kind of God-fearing friend who doesn't need details just that we have a burden and she will stop and pray then before long we both were praising and worshipping Him. Thank You, precious friend, sister in Christ, you always seem to know when to call me! I commented how I love Him and how strong His spirit is then she replied, "there ain't no limit on the distance" it was evident she was feeling that same Spirit, too.

I was later thinking how we speak with a feeble voice rather than with authority in Jesus name then we wonder why we can't feel Him and why our prayers feel useless! May these scriptures inspire you to weep, pray and praise allowing God to handle the situation. In Psalms 46:10 He tells us to "Be still and know I am God..." and in Isaiah 41:10 He said, "Fear thou not; for I am with thee: be not dismayed; for I am thy God: I will strengthen thee; yea, I will help thee; yea I will uphold thee with the right hand of my righteousness."

If you feel broken or burdened today, steal away with Jesus and feel that power and love that only He can give. Regain control and authority. Speak with boldness and confidence through Christ! Afterwards, add your answered prayer to your box of answered prayers for encouragement, so the next time Satan tries to open the gate to your playground you can prove once again He is a liar, deceiver, and discourager.

I spoke of taking authority away from the devil. Here is just another example of how that works. My youngest son had clicked on a sight on the internet that was demonic. He couldn't communicate his questions, so he was watching the video. When I saw what he was watching on that I-pad screen, I demanded he turn it off! He refused to cooperate, and I refused to back off. I knew I had to handle the situation in a way without causing more frustration. Then, right on time the scriptures about authority came to my mind and I began praying and anointing his room beginning at the doorway and continued all the way to where he was. I mean I was praying, like a woman unashamed to pray! When I got over to where he was, I opened my eyes and there he was handing over the I-pad to me. Oh, the power of prayer...

Luke 1:37, 6:21,47, 8:39, 10:17,19, 12:7, 14:27, 18:27, 22-32; Mark 11:22-26; Isaiah 41:10; Jeremiah 32:27; Hebrews 4:16; 1 Peter 5:7; Phill. 4:7; Ephesians 6:11; II Cor. 12:9-10; Acts 6:29, 16:31; II Cor. 10:4

~~~

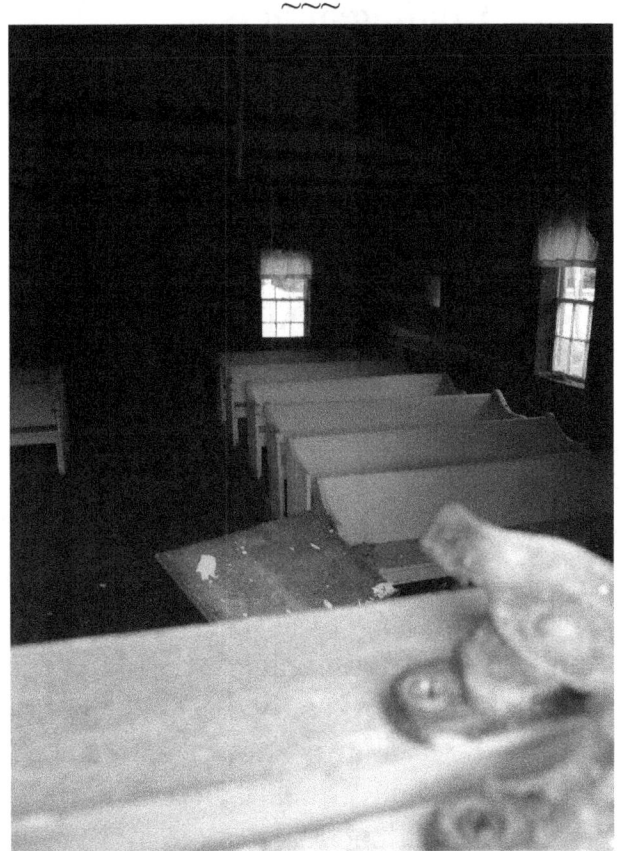

"Lookin' from the outside in… through a broken pane".

Jesus looks past our outside at our brokenness and pain, then renews our inner being! Praise His Holy Name!!!

~~~

Letting Go of the Denomination, Holding onto God

Once we learn it is no longer about us but all about Him, our lives are forever changed …our purpose, our goals, our unconditional vow! When we fully surrender, even if we must take this walk alone (being single), we are setting an example or precedence for others to follow. We will be held accountable!   SINCERITY MATTERS…

I do not argue with people about praying in an unknown tongue and I do not boast about this gift to others. Some of you may totally disagree with what you are about to read which is okay, I did not write this to be argumentative. He said to work out your own salvation with fear and trembling, found in Philippians 2:12-14. We are all given gifts, and this is only one of them, not saying this is the least gift. I never understood this gift before and never heard anyone in the church I regularly attended, speak in an unknown tongue. A lot of people put emphasis on this gift.   They seem to think one has a closer walk if they have this gift. I will leave that decision up to you, however we are not to be haughty or prideful as found in Proverbs 6:12,17,18.

The gifts are for edifying the Church, not for us to boast of. Remember we never earned them through a merit system! I Cor. chapters 12 through 14 speak of the gifts also in Romans chapter 12 we read of the gifts. Verse 6 of that chapter tells us "Having gifts differing according to the grace that is given to us..." Therefore, we understand He does not give us these gifts because we deserve them but only because of His grace. If we meditate on His goodness in our lives, we will see we all have been given gifts. Now, let's refrain from being jealous or boastful. In the book of Isaiah 11:2-3 we read of seven gifts. Acts 2:38 "Then Peter said unto them, Repent, and be baptized every one of you in the name of Jesus Christ for the remission of sins, and ye shall receive the gift of the Holy Ghost." I believe the interpretation of this scripture causes confusion however in I Cor. 14:33 "For God is not the author of confusion, but of peace, as in all churches of the saints." I have talked to folks who say they were given the gift of tongues as a babe in Christ and I do not dispute their word. I do believe if we want to be used of God, we are to put God first and seek to be close to Him, desiring His will in every facet of our lives, searching our lives for idols, sinful natures, or any wedges keeping us from having a closer walk with Him. We already read where the gifts are given by His grace. Our desire to serve and live a Godly life involves doing all we can to show Him we are sincere. The fruits of the spirit, as well as the gifts are more evident as we mature in the Lord. James 1:5 says if any lack wisdom let him ask of God, that giveth to all men liberally. 1 Cor.14 talks about tongues and verse 19 says, He would rather us speak five words in a known tongue rather than ten thousand words in an unknown tongue causing confusion. That is why I feel there should be an interpreter which is verse 5 (unless we are praying in tongues). Acts 2:4 speaks of utterance, "And they were all filled with the Holy Ghost, and began to speak with other tongues, as the Spirit gave them utterance." If I am not mistaken the word utterance is an unknown sound between the person and God that Satan cannot understand or interpret.

Sometimes after praying I may not know what the meaning of that utterance was, although sometimes He will reveal to me by replying with an answer then exchanging peace for the burden

I once felt. I do know how humbling I feel afterwards. It seems as though, when my heart is really heavy and I am crying out from the deepest part and cannot find the words to express myself, that is when I begin praying in an unknown tongue or utterance. Although that is not always the case. Wikipedia defines "utterance as a continuous piece of speech beginning and ending with a clear pause".

Years ago, when I was at sis' apartment, a time when our family was going through a horrific battle, I got down to pray and all I could do was make sounds. That is when I began praying in tongues. Then after that I did some but in the past few years even more. God knows when we are seeking a serious relationship with Him! I love to be in Churches when someone stands up and speaks and someone else interprets, there is a period of silence, then the interpretation comes. WOW, I love that! Some churches I hear a lot of praying in tongues and it used to be confusing. I wondered but praying is different than speaking to the Church...refer to 1Cor 12:28 and chapter 13.

I spoke with one of my Christian sisters about the confusion and misunderstanding I had been feeling. She was very helpful and rather than be boastful or confuse anyone, she informed me that we have the power to control the volume unless God has a purpose for the Church. Therefore, if I feel led to pray in a Church that does not practice praying in tongues, I do not want to quench the spirit nor confuse others; I turn the volume down.

If you have ever danced in the spirit, WOW what an experience! Here is an example: Once, I was really hurt by someone; honestly, I was not listening to the Holy Spirit. I had allowed myself to take the lead away from the Holy Spirit, thus ended with a broken heart. I was truly thankful for the Lord's compassion and the dance! I was standing by the washer in our home and danced, danced, and continued dancing until I was worn out. Someone would have thought I was crazy but after all that dancing I was relieved and felt such peace over the situation and the hurt I had once felt. God's timing is not always our timing. Later, Sid and I did go out a few times only as friends though and he was always such a gentleman. We have since remained good friends.

Later, there were times sis and I would be praying/worshipping in her room. I would begin to dance, and just could not stop. It may sound silly but sure was a wonderful spiritual feeling afterwards, even though I would be worn out physically. There have been other occasions God gave me a dance and I wish I could explain this but there are no words. The best way I know how to tell you is, He knows when we need spiritual strength, confirmation, rejuvenation, comfort and joy.

Another example was one night at Church when an evangelist was praying over Curt and the spirit was so strong, I couldn't stand still. I had never "danced" in a Church building before until that night. Later I realized I had received healing that night! These examples are facts one doesn't have to be in a Church house to feel the Holy Spirit. Even though we need to go there to worship and gain strength. At one time I was very faithful in attendance, but recently I haven't been able to go due to circumstances. Let me tell you, He is with us wherever we are!!!

Then there was The Run! That was an experience I never dreamed I would ever have. I am the kind of person who likes to take the back seat, but when God said, move, I knew I had to obey! When I ran in church that night, I gained so much strength that only can come from God; not physical strength, but spiritual strength. While few, if any, people knew what I was facing, God knew. He knew the daily struggle was real to me. I was caring, for my son, who has differing abilities, and for my sister who has cancer. I was also trying to be a mom to my other children, a nanna, and a help to my parents. Also, a sincere friend to others. I was overwhelmed and God knew it! I remember that night so well! I was surrounded by my family and Church family, yet felt alone, as if I was walking through the mountains and had gotten caught in a web within the path I was on. To some, it was probably quite a sight to see, a forty-nine, year old, overweight woman running through the church, but I did not care who was there or who was not. When I heard Him say, "Go"! I had to get out of that pew and go immediately! I wish I could explain the feeling of "rest" I had mentally after that small act of obedience.

Different people have asked me about these topics and some of you may still be reluctant, I would suggest you pray and study your Bible seeking wisdom. I'm no scholar, but I do know how God strengthened me when I was weak. I have so much yet to learn and I admit that.

1 Thes. 5:19 "Quench not the Spirit."

1 Thes. 5:22 "Abstain from all appearance of evil."

Ephesians 6:6-19; 1 Peter 4:11; 1 Cor. 12:28; 1 Cor. 14:28;

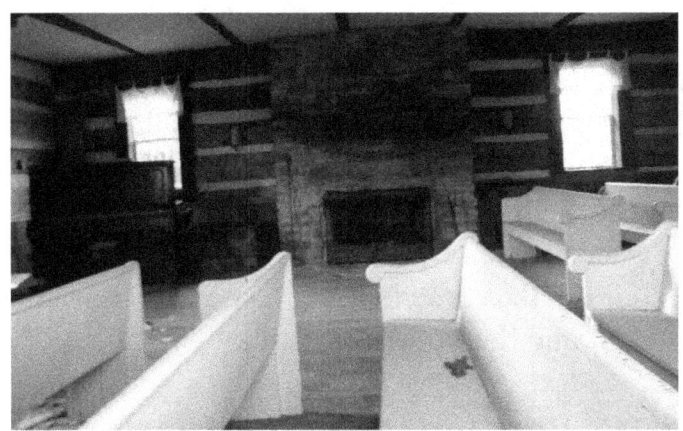

"The Heart of the Church… "

These last two photos were taken of a Church, while out of state, when the youth group from Church was on an outing. As I look at this picture, my mind wonders: What the sermons may have been like and their titles? Of all the prayers that were called out on bended knees, especially by those praying mothers/fathers. The healings that took place, and all those who were faithful despite their load. Can you imagine what the worship service was like? I wonder how many white hankies waved in the air and how many sang off key but did not care? If our country may have been at war during this era, or how many prayer warriors were shouting their victory during these services? Remember the scripture, He is the same yesterday, today and forever...Compare this to Churches today, we sit in padded pews, with thermostat-controlled heat and air, even have carpet and a sound system. But I wonder where is the Holy Spirit now? Some Churches are even closing their doors. If there ever was a time the Church doors need to be open, or a time we need to be *the Church*, that time is now! Date this church was built and the builder are unknown.

~~~

Pray for Discerning Spirits
(which is also a gift)

One night after Church, Curt and I went to town to grab a bite to eat. He used his picture card to tell me he wanted to eat at a specific restaurant. Not an expensive place, but where we eat from time to time. For some reason I felt uneasy about going there this time but dismissed the thoughts. Church ended later than usual that night so there was not a lot of patrons there. For some reason I kept hearing this Voice telling me to be on guard.

We got our food and due to Curt's choking hazard, I like to either eat inside, or park and wait for him to eat. Again, I heard that Voice telling me to be on guard, that someone was going to approach our vehicle. This is difficult to write without tears and chills! I began eating but was more observant to our surroundings, for this Voice was not backing off. I had just finished eating and was waiting for Curt when I happened to see someone in my side mirror approaching our vehicle. Thank God, I was smart enough to leave the car running but had put the gearshift in park. I gently moved the gearshift to reverse and by that time she was next to my window. I began backing out and as I did, I saw the person in the car across from us pointing at the restaurant across the road from us and she began walking to them and got in the backseat. I pulled out and they pulled out behind us leaving their lights off. I did not know what to expect but did know God was protecting us! That car followed us through two red lights then pulled off at a different restaurant. Yes, anyone could forget to turn their lights on in a city at night, I agree. However, I believe He gave me the gift of discerning spirits, warning me that evil was present, and I have thanked Him over and over for His protection once again!

~~~

Be Courageous

Have you ever told your child or children, "You can do this! I have faith in you, knowing they can do the task at hand"? We as parents, know our children can do whatever the task is we have given them. Even though they may not feel confident, capable, or adequate enough, to do that particular task. Yet we know, beyond a shadow of a doubt, they most certainly can handle it. Then later when the task is complete, from the look on their face, the expression of excitement, surprise or amazement we want so much to say, "I told you so"! God used this example today to remind me to keep the faith, and stay focused, for He knows I can accomplish whatever it is He has given me to do or He would not have given that job to me. Therefore, I want to tell you, Be courageous in the task He has given you!

Isaiah 41: 6 "They helped every one his neighbor; and every one said to his brother, Be of good courage."

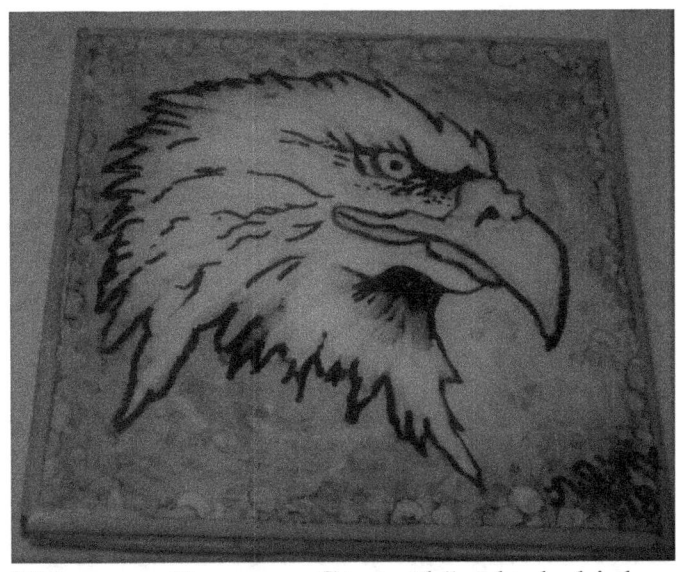

"Bravery...Courage...Strength" -alcohol ink

~~~

Spiritual Workout

Earlier today, as I was preparing for the walking trail, I was talking to the Lord about my heart's desire. During that time, I was meaning to say, I need a spiritual breakthrough! But the words escaped my mouth… I need a spiritual workout! I then chuckled knowing the soreness I felt from yesterday's walk, surely was not quite ready for a physical workout but how would a spiritual workout make me feel? I began to meditate on just what a spiritual workout would entail. Later while on the track, still meditating on the definition of a spiritual workout, I began to sing the old gospel song "Keep on the Firing Line". The words were powerful, almost as if the Lord was trying to tell me something through the verses in the song, just as if they coincided with a spiritual workout...."We must fight, be brave against all evil, never run or nor even lag behind. If we will win for God and the right just keep on the firing line...." Therefore, any workout whether spiritual or physical, in order to be successful, we must go at a steady pace, being consistent and dedicated, stay on track, and stay focused! We may sweat at times, get tired, thirsty (for living water), and meet folks along the trail. Sometimes with the same goal in mind and sometimes not. We MUST ingest healthy food (the Word) to keep our endurance and strength up for the workout. Rest is also important, but too much rest will lead to unhealthy habits!

I am amazed at the beautiful warm weather we are experiencing in February here today, seventy-seven degrees. That's just how God works. In the middle of a winter season He provides a week of warm, beautiful days, maybe because He knows we need a workout, spiritual and physical. When I think of all those dreary rainy days we have had, it was like being in a valley spiritually speaking. WHAT A

REFRESHER today has been!!! There may be more days ahead with snow and cold temperatures before spring finally breaks. May we not be slothful and forget the need to continue the most important workout, which is spiritual.

Lamentations 3:21-26; Romans 12:2, 8-21; Proverbs 18:9; James 1:22; James 2:18, 26; 1 Tim. 4:8

~~~

Less Time in the Kitchen and More Time in the Closet

Remember, an old children's book, in which there was a grueling sound coming from the closet? The moaning and groanings from the burden I felt today somehow reminded me of that book. When we are in our prayer closets, a child may think there is a scary being in our closets due to the sounds coming from there. The book teaches how to overcome fear. We as adults also have a book that teaches us how to overcome fear, the Bible! When we are faced with fear, we are to RUN... to our closets, *our prayer closets*. Not only then, but daily!

Today, as I was getting ready to eat, even though I was very hungry, I was in deep sadness or fear. You see, "the monster" had been placing snares in front of those I love! God spoke clearly, after hearing me cry out from the love I have for people who are going through deep valleys and fiery trials, to put my plate down right then and run to my prayer closet. The power of God was so strong. My agonizing cries were in desperation, and my need for Him to break these strongholds/chains were evident. After I had poured my heart out like a barrel of rain water, I felt Him speak these scriptures to me, "Be still and know that I am God..." Psalms 46:10 and in Jeremiah 29:11-13 "For I know the thoughts that I think toward you, saith the Lord, thoughts of peace, and not of evil, to give you an expected end. Then shall ye call upon me, and ye shall go and pray unto me, and I will hearken unto you. And ye shall seek me, and find me, when ye shall search for me with all your heart."

I believe we also read where "The Lord is nigh unto them that are of a broken heart..." Psalms 34:18.

Thank You, Lord for not only hearing my heart's cry but answering my cries! Parts of these scriptures came to me after praying that day. I then researched and found the scriptures and was even more amazed as I read the whole scripture-WHAT AN AWESOME GOD!!

Later that evening, I was determined to go to Church. We were late, but Oh... My...

Goodness, what a service we had! The closer I got to the building the stronger I could feel His Anointing. Yes, we were late but once inside, I could not quit shaking, even the preacher noticed when he and I shook hands upon Curt's and my arrival. I was not the only one feeling His Anointing... the singers were in harmony, the testimonies, the shouting and praising was unlike any other service I think I have ever been in. People were minding the Lord in such a way the preacher did not have to preach that night. I did not know if I was going to run, dance, shout or what, but I do know that feeling was real.

The people who had been on my mind earlier that day were there that night, and from the sight of them I knew God was working everything out for His Glory! I not only had to Praise Him for that, but for how I felt after praying today. I have never felt the Anointing that strong for that length of time. Even after I went to bed and recalled that service, I would begin shaking again. GOD IS REAL, HIS ANOINTING IS REAL!

I do not want to quench the Spirit, do you? Remember the white hankies the ladies used back in the day when they felt the Anointing? Reminds me of the white flag that was flown after a battle, a sign of surrender, metaphorically speaking. Maybe we need more white hankies in the House of God! A sign of our surrender to God. Remember the story of David and the giant? The battles we face are the Lord's, but the victories are ours through Him.

How do we handle the Holy Spirit? Do we allow him to move in our lives? Is He evident to others? Are we ashamed? Are we quenching the Spirit? I have been guilty in the past, too! Do you have a prayer closet? When was the last time you waved your white hankie? Our prayer closets should have a sign above the door, "NOT for Emergency Use only"! How devoted are we? Are we submissive or are we rebellious?

Matthew 6: 5-6 "...But thou when thou prayest, enter into the closet, and when thou hast shut thy door, pray to the Father in secret and thy Father which seeth in secret shall reward thee openly."

Acts 16:31 "And he said, Believe on the Lord Jesus Christ, and thou shalt be saved, and thy house."

Luke 12:40 "Be ye therefore ready also; for the Son of Man cometh at an hour when ye think not."

Luke 18:4 "I tell you, this man went down to his house justified rather than the other; for everyone that exalteth himself shall be abased; and he that humbleth himself shall be exalted."

Psalms 18:35; I Sam. 17:1-47

Luke 22:31 "And the Lord said, Simon" (I place my name here so as to say, N... rather than Simon) "Simon" (N...), "behold, Satan hath desired to have you, that he may sift you as wheat: But I have prayed for thee, that thy faith fail not: and when thou are converted, strengthen thy brethren." Once again... STRENGTHEN THY BRETHREN!

Why do we bother going to our prayer closets?

* Have we had a power surge and needed strength?

* On behalf of another needing prayers answered, healing or perhaps a miracle?

* To hold conversation with God, that is only to be kept within those walls?

* For direction, guidance, peace and/or comfort, intervention?

* For thanksgiving, a time for expressing our gratitude or to count our blessings?

* For some alone time with Christ, a time of pushing away everyone and everything else aside and meditate.

* To cry out in desperation?

* To bask in His Glory?

* To do a soul check?

* Most importantly, to worship Him?

All of these we probably have purposed in our hearts as we entered our prayer closets. Often-times we do all the speaking as if we are placing an order. How many times or how often do we stay there until we hear a word, an answer, a scripture or scriptures, or confirmation? What if all our conversations with others were always one sided, not allowing the other to answer or speak? This is a somber time, no doubt when tears are streaming down our faces and our hearts are heavy, the connection between us and Christ knowing He is the only one who can intervene.

Let's think of stories from the Bible where prayers were not only heard but answered. Like the lady who was diseased with an issue of blood for twelve years, touching the hem of His garment, her faith made her whole. (Matthew 9:20-22). Or the man at the pool who had an infirmity for thirty-eight years. He had not even gotten into the water and was healed because of his faith. (John 5:5-9). The boy healed from the point of death. (John 4:47-54). Elias who prayed for no rain for a specific number of days and then prayed the rain would come. (James 5:17). Remember when Jonah went to Nineveh?

The people prayed, and God changed His mind, and did not destroy the city. (Jonah 3:10). Remember also the man's hand that was restored? (Matthew 12:13). Do you recall because of the mother's faith, her daughter was made whole? (Matthew 15:28).

Do you have stories where miraculous healings took place, or your prayers were answered? Do you share them with others? I can think of the times He woke me in the middle of the night to pray. Sometimes, I would be so sleepy, and I admit I did not always obey. The times I did pray and later saw why the prayers were needed. What a humbling feeling that was. These were lessons He was teaching me on the importance of prayer. Sometimes, I would not always know why I was praying, but most of the time within the next few days I would soon find out. From those times I learned there was a reason He was waking me up to pray. Several instances were for protection of my family members from dangerous situations that I had no clue of until later.

Some examples were like the time the cliff fell onto the road below where my son had planned to travel on but later decided he needed to go the other direction without any knowledge the cliff was about to fall. Also like the time the houses on both sides of my daughter were broken into and she was spared. There are so many more examples...

Matthew 18:6 tells us "But whoso shall offend one of these little ones which believe in me, it were better for him that a millstone were hanged about his neck, and that he were drowned in the depth of the sea." I firmly believe we are to teach children to do good, sharing God's love by the examples we are setting, rather than promoting evil. Matthew 6:24 tells us "No man can serve two masters: for either he will hate the one, and, love the other; or else he will hold to the one, and despise the other. Ye cannot serve God and mammon." Where are we lacking in teaching children about Christ? What kind of example are we being? Are we teaching them the importance of time in our prayer closets by our examples?

Matthew 11:28 "Come unto me, all ye that labour and are heavy laden, and I will give you rest."

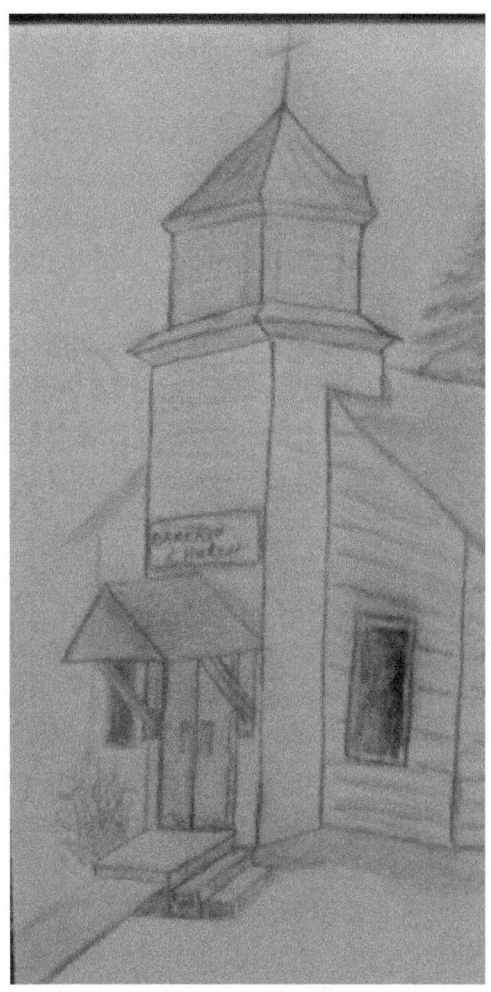

Sketch of the old Dameron Church that once was a well-known landmark, builder of the church unknown.

~~~

Spiritual Resources, Are We Using Them?

Do you ever get frustrated with yourself? I know I do! Aren't you glad Jesus is patient with us? Again, I KNOW I am! We are given an abundance of spiritual resources, yet do not use them adequately. We then wonder why we feel deflated or weary. Mark 9:29 tells us to pray and fast; and in Luke 9:1 we read, "Then he called his twelve disciples together, and gave them authority over all devils, and to cure diseases." Luke 9:23 tells us "...if any man will come after me, let him deny himself, and take up his cross, and follow me." Luke 10:19 "Behold, I give unto you power to tread on serpents and scorpions, and over all the power of the enemy: and nothing shall by any means hurt you." Verse 20 "Notwithstanding in this rejoice not, that the spirits are subject unto you; but rather rejoice, because your names are written in heaven." What is the difference between the disciples and us?

All throughout the Bible we find resources. Many have been referenced thus far. It is up to us to use them if we want a closer walk with Christ, a more powerful testimony, and boldness to proclaim His word. We all encounter or have encountered what we feel are extremely difficult tasks, or at some point a great deal of hurt...we MUST persevere! How are we to persevere? Praying, reading, studying, meditating, fasting, singing, renewing our minds daily, maintaining good works, and seeking His will in our lives. Titus 3:5 tells us "Not by works of righteousness which we have done, but according to his mercy he saved us, by the washing of regeneration, and renewing of the Holy Ghost; verse 6. "which He shed on us abundantly through Jesus Christ our Savior." Hebrews 5:16 "Let us therefore come boldly unto the throne of grace, that we may obtain mercy, and find grace to help in the time of need." If we back up to verse fifteen, we read, where Jesus was in all points tempted like we are, yet without sin.

Therefore, in verse four of the same chapter we read we are not to harden our hearts when we hear His voice. How often do we ignore His voice? How often do we use these spiritual resources in our daily lives? Hebrews 6:10-15 tells us God is not unrighteous to forget our works and labors of love which we have shewed forth in His name, ministering to the saints and yet still ministering. He tells us in verse 11 and 12 to hold on to that hope until the end, being not slothful but by keeping our faith and patience we will inherit the promises.

A few scriptures after these I read of how Abraham obtained the promise after He patiently endured. May we never lose sight of our promise either! In the book of James, he tells us that the trying of our faith worketh patience, and if we lack wisdom we are to ask of God not wavering. (James 1:3,5). For "a double minded man is unstable in all his ways." (James 1:8). We can use these resources in a variety of ways. What are some of the ways you will be using them? What resources are we lacking in having a more productive spiritual life?

Matthew 17:20 "And Jesus said unto them, Because of your unbelief: for verily I say unto you, If ye have faith as a grain of mustard seed, ye shall say unto this mountain, Remove hence to yonder place; and it shall remove; and nothing shall be impossible unto you."
Ephesians 5:19

~~~

A Lesson on "Time", "On Time"

I suppose being a mother of an adult child with differing abilities has impacted my life in such a way that I may take a different perspective or approach on things. I was thinking of the miraculous healings that took place in the Bible. Many sermons have been preached using this example and YES, Jesus is worthy of our Praise! I am sure the man who was healed was telling everyone of his gratitude toward Jesus.

After hearing a sermon one night I began to wonder what the man's life must have been like for the thirty-eight years prior to his healing. The passage tells us he had no one to put him in the water when the water was troubled although, on the day of his healing, he never entered the water. Jesus told him to take up his bed and walk! What an awesome sight that must have been, especially for his mother! As I have said, I have heard different sermons concerning this man who was lame and the one speaking will give his or her view of why the man didn't get in the water himself by possibly rolling or sitting closer to the pool. We do not know why, therefore the important element here is, time! I believe the length of time he was lame plays a great deal in this story for we learn no matter how long someone is lame or mute or deaf, Jesus can heal giving us hope our loved ones will be healed.

I also think of the people we have met since my son Curt was born. The people that have touched our lives making us better people, the lives he has touched, and the testimonies of how God brought him through numerous scary situations. We can do all we can, but the time for when healing is to take place is up to God. Some are healed miraculously, some are healed over time, it's all in His timing. I think of my other children and how God healed them at different times from when their fevers were spiking in the middle of the night, to other health issues they have faced.

Let's go back prior to the healing of the man who could not walk. I see first-hand how people are treated in the world today. Yet look how far we have come. I can't help but wonder how this man was treated! I wonder, had others given up hope on him, had he given up on himself? I wonder, did he minister all those years, in, spite of his condition? I wonder was he shunned or pushed aside because of his differences? There are many questions that may arise while reading. However, we are given enough scriptures to know we can trust the Lord's plan.

In Heaven, we will no longer need the aide of communication devices, wheelchairs, visually impaired assistance, advocates... The why's or how's, the stares, or the need for a healing. For some reason this story led me back to the classroom on advocacy.

Have you ever thought about when Jesus said to the man who was lame, "Rise, take up thy bed, and walk." (John 5:8) how that could relate to our lives? Have you ever allowed hurt or a situation to keep you from walking upright and strong?
John 5:5,6

~~~

Good Morning, God!

A day or two after I had prayed wanting confirmation that I was where I should be at this point in my life, just before awakening God clearly spoke scriptures for me to read. I was reassured I was there, at the destination, at the significant part of His plan; then a sense of relief overshadowed me! In the eyes of others my day may have looked stormy, but within I was at peace. Thank You God for Your awakening Voice...for Your reassurance!

~~~

Bless Those Who Throw Poo at You!

You may find a little humor in this story I am sure, however, no matter what the world throws at you, "BLESS THEM". Today has been one of those days where I could have easily thrown my hands up and just called it quits, allowing the devil to defeat me. One of those days where everything seemed to be going wrong, or maybe not so much the way I had planned or hoped. Then, throughout the day I was reminded several times of a dream I had just before awakening.

There is a scripture in Matthew 5:44 which we referenced earlier that tells us to bless rather than to curse someone. By doing so we are reminding Satan to whom we belong. I woke up feeling empowered, for in my dream I was standing in someone's house who was well known and popular. The longer I was there more and more people began appearing in the room. I began praying over people and prophesying. I knew there were people there who needed salvation. The Holy Spirit was so strong on me I was boldly proclaiming Christ and was not fearful or ashamed.

Later, we were outside on a street and a great deal of people were there along with much chaos and noise like one would hear in the city. Then I looked over and there were some men cleaning out a drain which was a septic line but for some reason it was coming out from the side of a brick wall. I turned and walked up another street and someone picked up some of that "poo" and threw it on me. Within myself I really wanted to retaliate, pick it up and throw it back at that person. I could feel anger and embarrassment, becoming more furious. In my mind I was making a horrendous choice to slam them with it! Right then the Holy Spirit spoke so clearly and precisely, saying "NO, Bless them instead!"

That was just what I did and throughout the rest of the dream, no matter what anyone did I would "Bless them". People would look at me in amazement and from the looks on their faces they knew something was different about me. I continued to speak with power and clarity surprising myself. It was as if the Holy Spirit was hovering over me like a cloud as I was walking along.

After awakening, I too, was amazed and in awe of how God could use someone like myself, knowing how imperfect I am and how backward I am. Several days after the dream, I was still reminded to "Bless" people and pray for them no matter how they treated me. I believe God knew what was coming my way and allowed this dream to remind me to be an example no matter what people throw at me, how bad it may hurt or how ugly they may make me look, whether it be words to belittle me or actions to tempt me.

May we always remember there are two sides to every story! I choose not to belittle others but rather take my hurt, anger and resentment to the Lord when being slammed with "poo" where it is not retold nor distorted. We all know how gossip is like a snowball effect. The words get turned and twisted with the more area it covers. May we give grace to others for it is through God's grace we are forgiven! I too have said things to people I thought were trustworthy, seeking advice, then later I learned my words hurt another, even though that was not my intention ...another lesson learned on trust and forgiveness. Remember...Bless Them No Matter How Much Poo We Are Slammed With! Remind me, Lord, to keep a watch on my mouth!

Luke 6:28 "Bless those who curse you and pray for those who spitefully use you."

Hebrews 13:6 "The Lord is my helper, I will not fear. What can man do to me?"

Philippians 6:10 "Finally my brethren, be strong in the Lord, and in the power of his might."

Proverbs 20:19; Ephesians 3:13, 16-21; 1 Cor. 10:13; 11 Cor. 12:9; 1 Peter 2:20; 1 Peter 4:15-16; 1 Peter 5:5; Romans 9:31; Romans 12:14,17-21; Romans 15:16; 1 Peter 3:16,17;

Col. 3:13; James 1:26; Acts 2:17; Psalms 41:9-13

~~~

A Special Calling?

Holidays can sometimes be difficult!! This year, just before Valentine's Day, I began a study of singles in the Bible. We tend to forget just because they were written about in the Bible, they were still human beings with feelings and needs. How long has it been since you were hugged with a confirming hug that told you, you were loved? Remember good touch, bad touch? Well, I am referring to a good hug. It is within norm, of the human race, to want to have a hug from the opposite sex, someone you love. This does not mean any and every man, but an occasional hug from someone dear to you. The hug is meaningful to that relationship! I started to research the effects of hugs while on this topic but didn't. However, I do remember as a teacher how important it was to kids to get a hug every day. I also remember in my dating years and into my marriage how important it was to have a hug, a sign of confirmation I was accepted and loved.

We read of women and men in the Bible and wonder about their daily lives and their loneliness. We also read of how they were busy with the Lord's work. We must be careful that passion, lust, loneliness, or desperation doesn't take us down a road we may not want to find ourselves on. We must be careful with hugs too! (sarcasm inserted)

Some are not brave enough to discuss, therefore shy away from, what seems a taboo topic, celibacy. This is making the conscious choice to abstain from sex until married, remember the scripture in 1 Cor. 7:34? In, today's society, this is a subject some scoff at, not a well perceived topic. Just maybe we need to apply our talents and energy, devoting more time to the Lord's work rather than being self-consumed. Sometimes, being single or a widow for an extended amount of time feels like we are rated second class, although it shouldn't. Many times, we avoid gatherings or social events if we have to go alone. We also must be able to balance our time, for too much time alone can give one the title of an "introvert", allowing the devil to inject negative feelings of low self-esteem where they don't belong. He will also try to convince us that we are not worthy of a significant other. He is a liar!

We sometimes, as singles/widows and even bachelors, are placed in a separate category by wives or husbands. They suspect we are out to sabotage their marriages when that never crossed our minds at all. I personally have developed friendships with both males and females. As a woman of God, I tend to have conversations with males and females alike. I firmly disagree with adultery, and fornication, and do encourage closeness in marriages! I see males as well as females who are longing to be understood and loved within their marriages.

Do you ever think of being single as a special calling on your life? Whether the time be short or lengthy, with God's grace we can rise up to that calling! Do you remember reading where the Lord told Jeremiah not to marry? (Jeremiah 16) He may have married later, I am not sure, I have not studied enough to know that answer, but I found that interesting!

We can look at some marriages and sigh a breath of relief we are not in that kind of relationship. Then we see other marriages and wonder, why we are still single? Wishing spouses were appreciated more! Whatever the reason, I have learned there is much needed ministry work to be done... the harvest is plenteous but the labourers are few. (Mathew 9:37,38). I do hope one day to have a husband who I can work alongside in the ministry, but for now I will continue His work one day at a time...

We read of Dorcas, also known at Tabatha, who was a widow in the Bible. (Acts 9). This lady was a fine example of compassion. Then we read of Naomi and her daughter in law Ruth; in the book of Ruth. Let's not forget Anna who was about eighty-four years of age. A widow for many years never departing from the temple, fasting and praying night and day; in the gospel of Luke.

We read in I Timothy 5 of the widow and of the young widow. In that same chapter we read where the young widow is to marry and have a family rather than be spoken of reproachfully.

Let's stop and think what we have been through thus far in our lives...if we have been through something traumatic, such as a death of a spouse or a divorce, possibly a lengthy separation, or whatever we have faced. We can use that to relate to someone a little differently than someone who hasn't been through that situation. Therefore, I believe when we have a little more understanding our compassion level will be different. I do not see a lot of ministries within the churches geared toward singles. Often, we hear of couples' nights or youth night. What about singles' nights, where Christian

170

singles can get together and enjoy an evening sharing common goals or situations? Maybe it is because most of the leaders I have met are married or have families.

We read in the Bible where women have different roles as do the men. Whether we are married or not, we all have a job to do whether it be domestic duties, obligations with our families, or field work pertaining to ministry. Although, we all are to be under subjection to the Lord for we all have a calling on our lives, whether it's to be a witness by the daily life we lead, touch one soul at a time or many at once. We all have gifts and talents...let's use them to help another.

James 1:22-25; Acts 9:36; Jude 22; 1Cor. 7:8; Mat. 5:16, 19:12, 6:1; Ephes. 2:8-10; Titus 3:5 Jeremiah 17:7, 29:11; Deut. 7:3; Ecles. 4:6,11,12; Luke 2:36,37; Deut. 7:3; I Tim. 5; II Peter 3: 9-11,14,17,18; Hebrews 13:15,16; I Cor. 7:8, 32-35; II Cor. 6:14; I John 2:15-17; Psalms 27:14; Isaiah 41:10, 54:5; Hosea 2:19,20; Mark 12:25; Gen. 2:18; James 1:12-16; Rev. 7:17, 19:7

~~~

The Rabbit Hole

In this book, I've shared personal testimonies, thoughts and lessons learned, but we have not talked much about situations that overwhelm us, or the effects of heart wrenching news. These are things we do not like to discuss! Loneliness, sadness or hurt, can cause one to dig deeper into his or her shell, closing everyone out. I know I have been there, in a rabbit hole! Even church attendance was neglected. How can that be after all these writings of courage and perseverance?

One day I ran across an old newspaper article as I was starting the fire in our wood furnace. The article was well written and gave an example of how these people whom were stuck in a deep pit with no way out and the people at the top of the pit kept yelling for them to give up, and so they did. All except for one, who was deaf, and he finally got out since he couldn't hear their negativity. Therefore, no matter what negative voices we hear we must turn a deaf ear and keep striving. I later heard a sermon, of when we see people in the pit, we are to get in the pit with them. I pondered… What an interesting statement!

Let's stop for a minute and ask ourselves these questions. When we see someone who has made bad choices what do we do? Do we visit folks when they are in the pit, or if we even think they are near the pit? If so, is it out of curiosity, or is it out of pure love, or do we shun them, thinking we are above that? Do we pretend we do not know of any gossip concerning the mistakes someone has made? Are we hindering their path, or being a friend who genuinely cares, and guiding them back to Christ? Is there someone we haven't heard from in a while and need to love on? What sacrifices do we make visiting those who are hurting? Do we as Christians have a servant's heart caring for one another, extending mercy and forgiveness the way Jesus would? The way we would want someone to extend that mercy and forgiveness to us?

The past few months have not only been the darkest months of the year due to the equinox but have also been a dark time in my life. Many times, people have no clue when we are living in a rabbit hole per se, it seems I was in the desert facing one obstacle after another. Things I never dreamed would happen.

I hadn't talked to this dear friend in years and her phone call was perfect timing. Somehow, she knew I was in a pit or a *rabbit hole*. She is a sister in the Lord who lives several states away and very knowledgeable in scriptures. She is

eighty years of age, but still chugging along being mindful of God's will for her life, and evidently listening to that still small Voice that knew I needed a phone call. Let's just say she really knows how to uplift and inspire! She is not the kind of person who needs to know what is ailing a person, or why they are in a rabbit hole, only that she was sent to encourage, recall scriptures, and give examples of how God was with her during her own rabbit holes. After our conversation, I once again heard these words, "Don't let the hurt make you bitter".
Rejuvenated, I got ready and headed to church.

While at church, I found myself able to make conversation, but most of all I wanted to just stand once again in that pew and offer praises to my Lord for how He loved me through my darkest days. Just like the sun, He is still there even when those dark clouds block the view. I had been in such a state, I had dug so far back in my rabbit hole, that I didn't want to be around people and there was no light in sight.

Earlier, as we were talking, she said to me, "Don't let Satan clap his hands as if he thinks he has won by discouraging you". With that being said, I want to end this chapter encouraging you in the same manner...let's remind him who he is and WHO WE ARE! We are NOT going on any more guilt trips or to any more pity parties! May we be encouraged! May we be encouragers! Let's not just crawl out of that rabbit hole but jump with excitement, embracing life, welcoming the "Son-shine", and face uncertainty, knowing we are strengthened by our Lord. Oh, let's not forget to roll a stone in front of the rabbit hole door so there is no re-entry! Let's not allow the betrayal of those who we thought were our friends to dishearten us but show the world we are overcomers!

About a month had passed since my friend had called, then I received another call from her, and as our conversation went along, she said, "We have been praying for you, N...!". I was excited to respond, "God answered those prayers!"

I am grateful He hears our prayers and the pleas from others on our behalf! Several prayers have been answered since I was in that rabbit hole! People do not have to know the details of your supplications, just that we need strength to dig out from the hole we burrowed ourselves into.

We have heard Curt say several phrases since then, too. I am still claiming the scripture in Luke 18:27, for him.

What if I had stayed in that rabbit hole? WOW... sure glad I didn't, and so thankful for that phone call!!! Loving on people...MATTERS!

Ephesians 4:31, 32 "Let all bitterness, and wrath and anger, and clamour, and evil speaking, be put away from you, with all malice: 32. "And be ye kind one to another, tenderhearted, forgiving one another, even as God for Christ's sake hath forgiven you."

~~~

Escaping the Rabbit Hole

Do you have or want an intimate relationship with Christ? The more of life's calendar I check off, OH MY how I have learned the roots of my love for Christ have grown even deeper, especially during some of those days when I was given unexpected appointments with hurt. I learned that even in the rabbit holes, HE IS THERE! You know those times when it felt like you were sucker punched, leaving you flat on the ground, breathless? Those times when words felt like a ton of bricks to your heart that took days to realize what just hit you?

Now if we allow that hit that left us breathless on the ground to paralyze us, we may quit reading our Bibles. We may seclude ourselves in that rabbit hole by not attending Church among other things. We may become introverted, allowing the opinions of others or the assumption there of, thus allowing the devil to be happy.

When we stop reading, get discouraged, seclude ourselves, we allow betrayal to turn into self-pity. All, of these elements are distractions and are not healthy, mentally and spiritually.

Yes, we all have encountered hurt at some point in our lives and I admit some hurts can give a hard punch. But we must never lay down our road map! During this hurt I spoke of, I held tight to my Lord, for He was the only one who understood! I wanted a conversation with Him, sometimes one-sided and myself doing all the talking! I didn't want to discuss the matter with anyone else, I didn't even want to think of it, the deep sadness, the betrayal I felt, and the emotions were just too much. All I wanted to do was hide not physically, but mentally in a corner and be embraced with the kind of hug only Jesus can give, you know that kind with lasting comfort. If I had been more daily dedicated to reading, had devoted more time daily to prayer and worship, what a difference that would have made in my defense mode when that ton of bricks came.

We read we are not to forsake the assembling of ourselves together as we see the day approaching. We also read in John 3:13,14 we not only need to praise God continually and do good works, we also please God by communicating, which means listening as well as speaking. Good works are not only expected, but He longs for us to continually communicate with Him. How does doing good works fit in right here? Well, even though we may be facing giants, we can still share a few stones with others who are facing giants in their lives. Hurt teaches us to have compassion and to help others to be overcomers as well. When we free our hearts from distractions, we can be more receptive and more thoughtful of others. When we come in contact, with hurt, we then know He will embrace us once again like no other can. Then, with each hurt thereafter we know on whom we can depend. We also know we have matured in the Lord when we no longer wish bad things or want to hurt others with words or with retaliation who have hurt us or our family. No, we're not being cowards. We have learned to shake the dust off and shine for the Lord!

I not only received a physical healing but have since had an awakening to be more compassionate...from being in that deep dark pit, the rabbit hole, the times of struggling to make ends meet, and the undisclosed hurt, have all taught me to show compassion and seek a closer walk with God! For when we let that hurt turn to bitterness, we tend to spew harsh words out of our mouths...out of the abundance of the heart the mouth speaks. (Matthew 12:34). Let's Speak with Compassion and think from our hearts!!!

Hebrews 13:15,16, 12:1; Gal. 6:9; II John 3:13,14; I John 4:4; I Peter 4:16; James 1:3; I Peter 3:4; Matthew 12:34; Luke 6:45

~~~

Let Me Introduce You to my Best Friend

I have shared with you lots of different topics but the most important of all is how to receive salvation! You have read my testimony and He will love you the same way! I promise! We all fail! The good news is HE IS THERE...He will be there through your grieving, your silly moments, your parenting issues, your joyous times, and even in your rabbit holes...His name is JESUS!

The Plan of Salvation...is simple! *A*ccept Christ as your Savior, *B*elieve He died for you, *C*onfess your sins to Him. There are no specific words you must say, just a heart-felt confession. Then share your good news with others! Write your story!!!!!

John 3:16 "For God so loved the world, that He gave His only begotten Son, that whosoever believeth in Him should not perish, but have everlasting life."

Romans 10:9-13: "That if thou shalt confess with thy mouth the Lord Jesus, and shalt believe in thine heart that God hath raised him from the dead, thou shalt be saved. For with the heart man believeth unto righteousness; and with the mouth confession is made unto salvation. For the scripture saith, Whosoever believeth on him shall not be ashamed. For there is no difference between the Jew and the Greek: for the same Lord over all is rich unto all that call upon him. For whosoever shall call upon the name of the Lord shall be saved."
II Peter 9:3-18

~~~

Read Col. 3:23...lest we forget let's make it our goal to do all things as if we are doing them for the Lord.

~~~

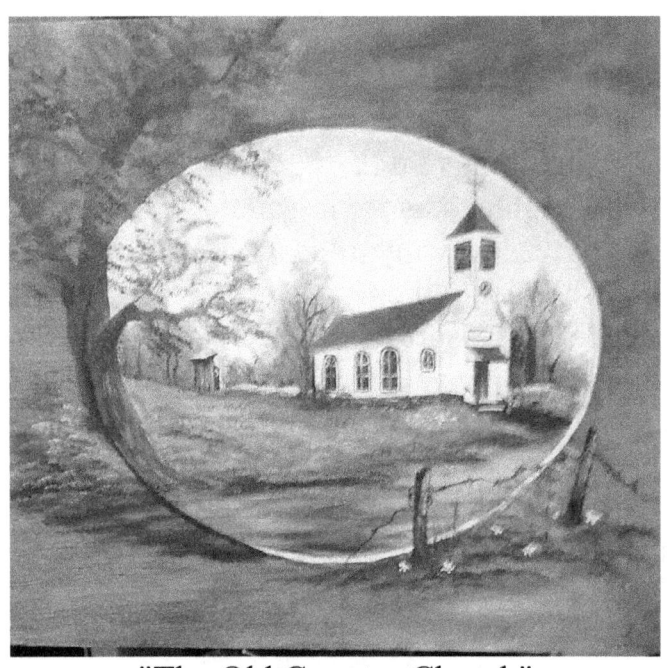

"The Old Country Church"
Thanks Marsha, for this photo. This was one
of my favorite paintings done in 1989. The
Church reminds me of the Church on Peach Tree
Road, and the church at Sylvester. There was a
total of three paintings done like this one;
original artist/designer unknown.

~~~

Mom's Do's and Don'ts

Don't waste your money on roses for my
casket but place a warm homemade quilt instead.
Then please give it to someone in need

as my last gift, in remembrance of the life I led.
   Don't weep bitter tears but laugh and smile
thinking of the funny things I said
and the silly things I did,
 let your laughter stay for a while!
   Don't give away my things grudgingly
nor selfishly hoard them away;
for Heavenly treasures
are of much more value, any day!
   Don't compare my life to anyone else's
for I was unique in God's eyes,
nothing to Him about my life
was taken by surprise!
He knew the choices I made,
whether bad or good,
I spent my last days serving Him,
He knew I would!
   Tell people, "Don't look down your nose as
you pass by
thinking she was just a mother, that is a lie."
Being a Mom and Nanna were her favorite jobs
but being a Christian was her greatest call!
Watching things unfold from the simplest act of
obedience were miracles she saw.
   Don't say my life was hard
while here on earth,
we all face challenges, that make us strong
and make us realize-Heaven's worth.

Don't sell our home
but rather keep the doors open
for those who need love, genuine and true.
Share the memories and open wide
the windows for new memories to blow through.
These are the things I would want you to do
or not do then plan to meet me again beyond the
blue!
Love, Mom

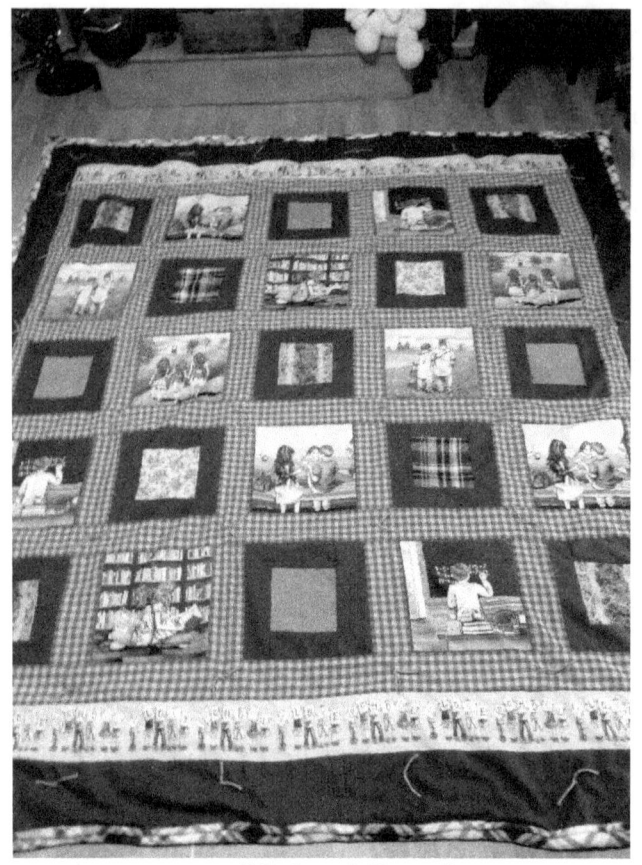

"School Days"
One of my favorite quilts; fabric designer
unknown; Quilting, a W.V. tradition

I Cor. 16:15; "...that they have addicted
themselves to the ministry of the saints."
II Cor. 9:7

~~~

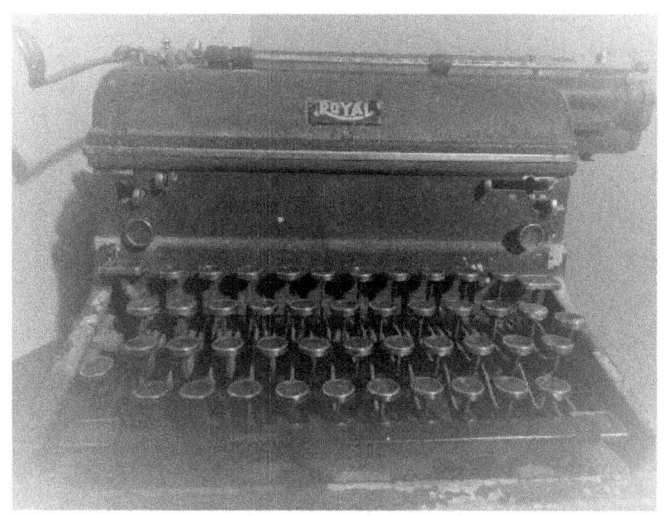

"Strike, Click…Ding!"

I can vividly remember using this as a child... The clicking sound of the keys as they struck against the red and black ink ribbons. The dinging sound, the bell made when the paper needed rolled to the next line. The careful attention needed to align the paper properly then rolling the paper through the machine. Liquid white out was used for mistakes, and those old keys was the first "keyboard" I typed on. I can't remember where mom and dad got this. I do, however, remember how excited I was to get to peck on it.

~~~

Me, an author...NO WAY!

It is still hard for me to believe that I am writing a book after all these years. Through the editing process I have come to realize why English class was so important. Wish I would have been more attentive! Mrs. W. would be shocked to see my name as author!!! As a child I hated to read. Later when I was a teacher people jokingly commented, "You do not have to write a book", referring to the lengthy notes in the children's files. This book began by collecting and compiling all my writings/art as a Christmas gift for my children. However, I felt the need to continue writing and learned writing can be very therapeutic and helpful to others facing the same circumstances.

The chapters in these books are related to the chapters in my life. I am still in awe of how some of these chapters were written and concluded not only in these books, but in my life. GEEZ...what learning experiences and spiritual growth, especially recorded in this book! When nearing the end, I was unable to find enough words to express my thoughts. I felt the books were complete and just needed edited. Thus, reading and editing was like opening a time capsule. I admit some stories were incredibly harder than others, so I had to take a break. I needed more time to allow God's healing to continue to restore me before finishing the books, especially Volume Three. Later, I found myself writing and sharing more, making this delay even longer. Three years later and we are now in the home stretch, EXCITED to see the final draft!

I have burnt the midnight oil many, many, nights writing, typing, and editing. I often found myself in the recliner with my Bible and our cat, Sabastian. He seemed to know the days/nights when my heart was the heaviest. Since I have had more time at home lately, I was able to pen some heartfelt feelings and record some memories I hope you enjoyed reading.

We see writers on television, usually being alone at a beautiful relaxed location. They are clicking away on their typewriter being able to concentrate fully on their thoughts, writing, then editing, and finally zipping the last paper out of the typewriter. Do not be misled, for Hollywood does not portray the life of every writer, especially as these books were written.

I became so engrossed in my writing, I stayed up very late many nights appreciating the silence and the calmness of no one requesting my time. By doing so, I avoided the distractions encountered during the day. Although, sometimes I was accompanied by my son, Curt, who was joyfully strumming his guitar, yet to learn what harmony and chords meant. Sometimes I would hear the birds beginning to sing as I was lying my head on the pillow, and on other days there were some early mornings I would arise before the busy day began. Some days, when I had a little time to devote to working on this or at least I thought I did, the phone would ring, or the dog would need to go outside, or the clock would remind me it was time to cook dinner. There were other times Curt would decide he would rather have my attention than to continue what he was previously doing. Also, to add a little humor, I must share how our old dog Jake, a yellow lab, would often lay near me with a full tank of gas. Some of these words or sentences were jotted down while sitting at a red light or waiting in doctors' offices.

The Lord has revealed Himself numerous times, especially when I was searching for answers to be able to come to grips with life's challenges. While searching, I found He truly does know me and loves me without hesitation! I have found a peace I cannot describe, a comfort incomparable, inner strength, and a boldness to speak His word. I learned humbleness and perseverance. To be able to keep silent when I feel like condemning people or blasting them with distasteful words when they have hurt me, also love and compassion, absolutely gifted from Him.

In each of the chapters, I have added stories throughout my time of editing these books. This is the bonus of having a computer versus a typewriter, although Volume One, contains my most recent writings. Every time I would pick up the rough draft and think now it was time to do the final edits, I would start a new story, study scriptures, and find myself excited for how Christ was speaking to me.

As I write from experience hoping to encourage someone who is in a similar situation to put their trust in the Lord. Writing has also helped in my healing. Is God pleased with how you and I are handling the challenges in our lives?

As you have read, and I hope you continue to read Volume Two and Three, how God inspired and worked through the chapters of my life, and as I write and edit, I can see a transformation from the person I used to be to the person I have become. In Volume Two, I have included a poem, "I Used to be Different".

Keep in mind some of the stories were written when I was not serving the Lord, I tried to note the ones that were written during that time (Mostly in Volume Two).

In Volume Two, you will read how mountain climbing was a physical challenge at times, just like spiritual mountains can be challenging. There have been some spiritual mountains which seemed impossible to reach the peak, although through all of the climbing I have become a learned woman with more compassion and love for mankind, with a stronger desire to be closer to God. May we find ourselves seeking to be closer to Him every day! No, we're not quite Home yet. Let's help each other make it there! May you be inspired to write and share your story!

I Cor. 15:58 "Therefore, my beloved brethren, be ye steadfast, unmovable, always abounding in the work of the Lord, forasmuch as ye know that your labour is not in vain in the Lord."

II Cor. 4:8,9,16, 18; 8. "We are troubled on every side, yet not distressed; we are perplexed, but not in despair. 9. Persecuted, but not forsaken; cast down, but not destroyed. 16. For which cause we faint not; but though our outward man perish, yet the inward man is renewed day by day. 18. While we look not at the things which are seen, but at the things which are not seen, for the things which are seen are temporal; but the things which are not seen are eternal."

II Cor. 12:9; "And he said unto me, My grace is sufficient for thee: for my strength is made perfect in weakness. Most gladly therefore will I rather glory in my infirmities, that the power of Christ may rest upon me."

II Cor. 6:4 "But in all things approving ourselves as the ministers of God, in much patience, in afflictions, in necessities, in distresses,"

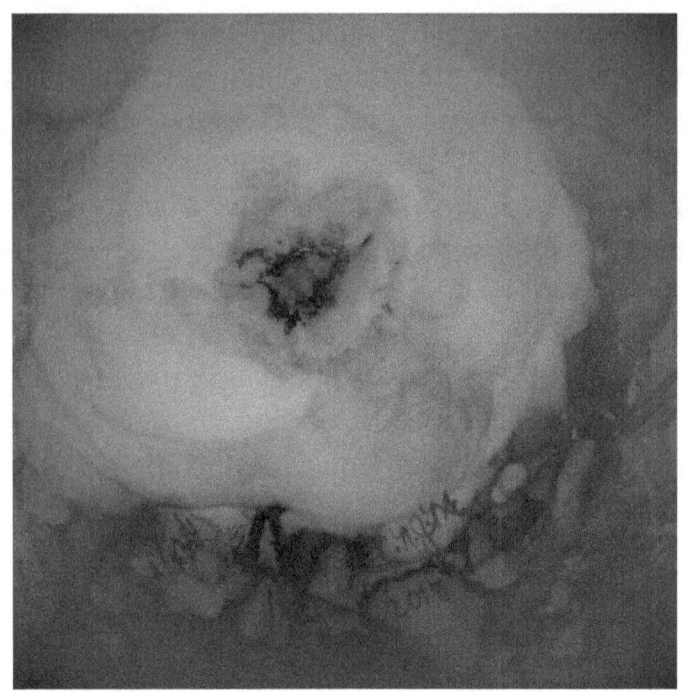

"An Unexpected Discovery"-alcohol ink

HOME...is in Sight!
We've Got to Make it…
...BECAUSE GETTING THERE,
MATTERS!!!

To be continued....

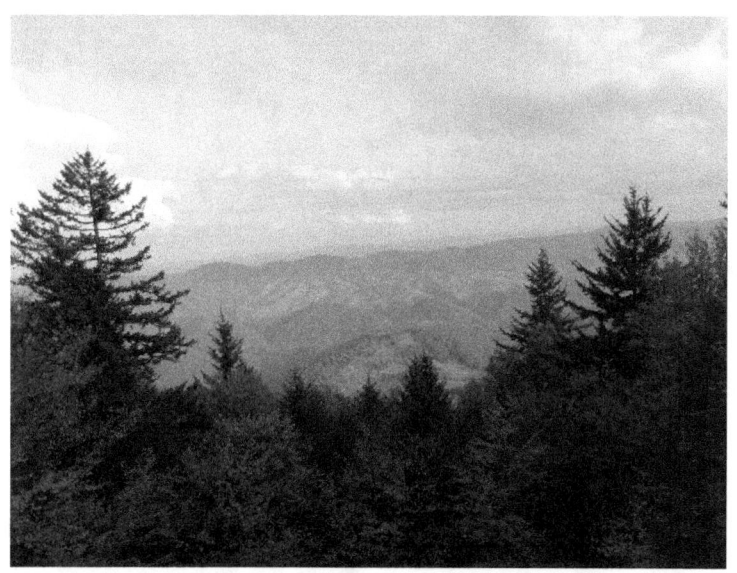

"Nearing the Summit" …Photo taken while
hiking in West Virginia.

Photography has been one of my favorite
hobbies since elementary school.

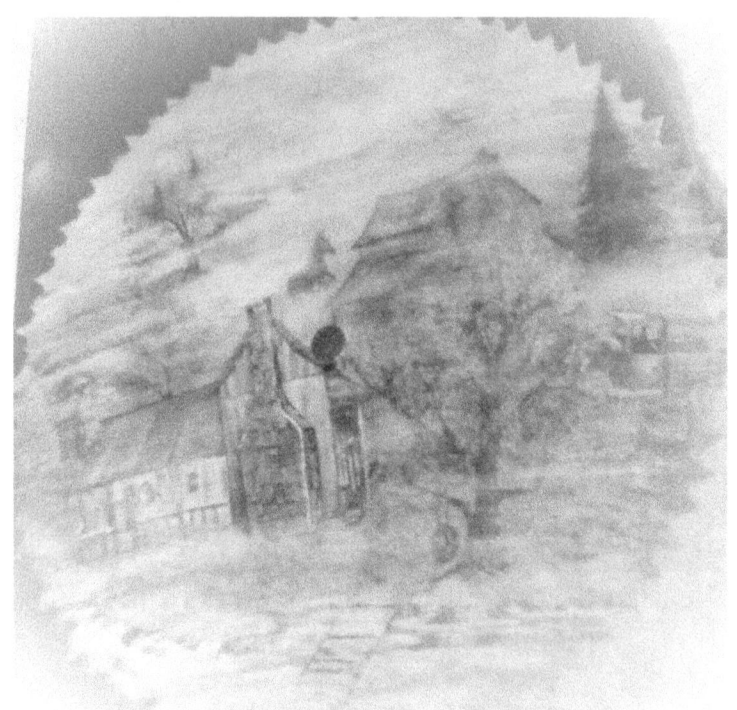

"A Misty Mornin' on the Farm"
Oil painting on a saw mill sawblade, original
designer/artist of the house unknown.

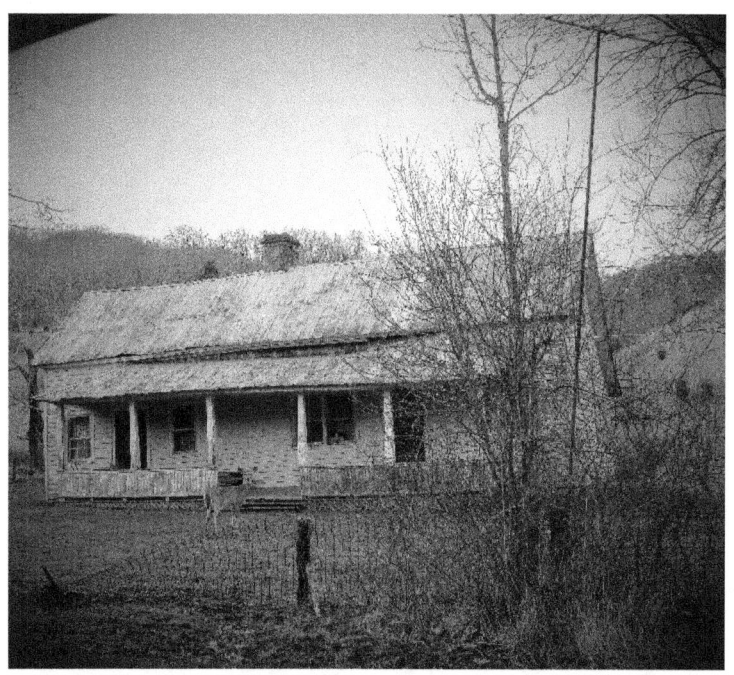

"The View" Photo taken during a Sunday drive on an old country road. Notice how the deer glares as if he or she has squatter's rights.

ABOUT THE AUTHOR

Nevaeh J.M. Sapphire was born a coal miner's daughter and raised in the Appalachian Mountains of West Virginia. She is the youngest of five children. Nevaeh married her childhood sweetheart, became the mother of three children and later the Nanna to three grandchildren. She obtained her Associate degree during the time she was rearing her children and working a full-time job as a preschool teacher. Once she became a widow at the age of forty-four her life began what she thought was a downhill spiral however one day at a time through Christ she learned who He really is and how His divine plan awakened her to spiritual growth. Absolutely was not the perfect dream life nor fairy tale but a place of peace and contentment which is far more valuable. Nevaeh enjoys simplicity, family time and the outdoors and much of her writing, poetry, art and photography include her love for these.

www.ingramcontent.com/pod-product-compliance
Lightning Source LLC
Chambersburg PA
CBHW060844170526
45158CB00001B/233